The Maltese Touch of Evil

Shannon Scott Clute
and Richard L. Edwards

DARTMOUTH COLLEGE PRESS

HANOVER, NEW HAMPSHIRE

THE MALTESE TOUCH OF

*Film Noir and
Potential Criticism*

EVIL

Dartmouth College Press
An imprint of University Press of New England
www.upne.com
© 2011 Trustees of Dartmouth College

Manufactured in the United States of America
Designed by April Leidig-Higgins
Typeset in Garamond Premier Pro by
Copperline Book Services, Inc.

University Press of New England is a member
of the Green Press Initiative. The paper used in
this book meets their minimum requirement
for recycled paper.

For permission to reproduce any of the material
in this book, contact Permissions, University Press
of New England, One Court Street, Suite 250,
Lebanon NH 03766; or visit www.upne.com

Library of Congress Cataloging-in-Publication Data
Clute, Shannon Scott.
The Maltese touch of evil : film noir and potential
criticism / Shannon Scott Clute and Richard L. Edwards.
p. cm. — (Interfaces: studies in visual culture)
Includes bibliographical references and index.
Includes filmography and podcastography.
ISBN 978-1-61168-047-8 (pbk. : alk. paper)
ISBN 978-1-61168-185-7 (ebook)
    1. Film noir — History and criticism. 2. Podcasting —
Study and teaching. I. Edwards, Richard L., 1965–
II. Title.
PN1995.9.F54C68   2011
791.43'6556 — dc23   2011038835

5 4 3 2 1

For our wives, Cathie and Sybil;
without you neither this nor any
other project would come to fruition.

And for our daughters, Tallulah, Vivienne, and Eve;
may you be more than a little hard-boiled.

Doit-on s'en tenir aux recettes connues et refuser obstinément d'imaginer de nouvelles formules? (Must one adhere to known quantities and obstinately refuse to imagine new formulas?)— François Le Lionnais, "LA LIPO (Le premier Manifeste)"

La lecture potentielle a le charme de faire ressortir la duplicité des textes, qu'ils soient oulipiens ou non. (*Potential reading* has the charm of making manifest the duplicity of texts, be they oulipian or not.)— Harry Mathews, "L'algorithme de Mathews" (emphasis ours)

On constraint: having to work within limits produces *formal* solutions with their own elegance and beauty. Wouldn't it be a bit philistine to point to the constraints of the sonnet as making it unlikely that the poet could produce satisfying work, having to keep to fourteen lines and a rhyme scheme? In media studies the outstanding example of formalist rehabilitation of elaborately constrained work has been our discovery of how very, very beautiful, whatever else they may be, the products of classic Hollywood studio system were. — John O. Thompson, "Dialogues of the Living Dead"

Contents

Acknowledgments

IF YOU ALLOW US here a moment of overwrought (but apt) metaphor, we promise to be straightforward in the body of this text. The road taken by most films noir winds through dark places—fog-shrouded, lonely, and full of dead ends. The road to creating this particular book on noir has been quite the opposite—a trip travelled from the beginning with a friend, a thoroughfare large enough to accommodate many fellow travelers, a place marked by numerous moments of illumination. This book is a "road map into the twisted world of noir" (as one of our listeners once said of our podcast series on the subject), and we hope it may provide many useful new inroads into the subject. But to get to this point, the latest stop on our noir journey, required direction from many parties and their encouragement to go beyond where the sidewalk ends.

First, we'd like to thank the academic mentors who opened the world of thought to us. We are truly privileged to have had so many generous mentors and colleagues who modeled for us the kind of close reading and interdisciplinary thinking we are pursuing here. For Clute, these include Richard Klein, Kathleen Perry Long, Tim Murray, Mitchell Greenberg, Tom Conley, Ester Zago, and Pamela Marcantonio, along with many others at University High School, the University of Colorado at Boulder, and Cornell University. For Edwards, these include David James, Marsha Kinder, Michael Renov, Dana Polan, Rick Jewell, Drew Casper, and Marita Sturken, along with many others at Loyola Academy, Wesleyan University, University of Chicago, and the University of Southern California. Special thanks go to Harvard professor Tom Conley, who provided both a substantial portion of the initial inspiration for this book (by way of a course he offered at Cornell University that taught us to visualize textual space in a more precise manner, and by way of his many excellent books on self-conscious language and space in literature and film) and invaluable suggestions for the final manuscript (right down to the level of helping us to navigate a particularly dicey bit of translation): "Qui ne voit que j'ay pris une route par laquelle, sans cesse et sans travail, j'iray autant qu'il y aura d'ancre et de papier au monde?"

Likewise, we would like to acknowledge the support and helpful suggestions we received from our colleagues at USC, the University of Kentucky, Saint Mary's College of California, IUPUI, Indiana University Bloomington, and Turner Classic Movies, especially Ed Tywoniak, Costanza Dopfel, Catherine Marachi, Claude-Rhéal Malary, Genevieve McGillicuddy, Scott McGee, and Heather Margolis. Special thanks to Shawny Anderson at Saint Mary's for her early support of our noir project and her generous efforts on our behalf to get podcasting recognized as scholarly activity, and Jeffrey Peters at UK, for his reasoned defense of the importance of our podcasting scholarship and for the opportunities he supplied us to demonstrate the pedagogical applications of our podcast methodology. We would also like to thank Kristi Palmer and IU Libraries for their support of our podcasts, and those at the Institute for Digital Arts and Humanities in Bloomington, who are working with us on the MTOE Database Project, especially Ruth Stone, Suzanne Lodato, and Will Cowan. And our gratitude goes to Bryan Alexander, codirector of the Center for Educational Technology at Middlebury College, for his unflagging support of our podcasting efforts, and Jared Case of the George Eastman House for his insights into our podcasts and this book.

We'd also like to thank the many authors, filmmakers, and scholars who have participated in, or provided feedback on, our two podcast series, which were the building blocks of this project: *Out of the Past: Investigating Film Noir* and *Behind the Black Mask: Mystery Writers Revealed*. In particular, we'd like to thank Megan Abbott, an accomplished scholar of film noir and hard-boiled writer extraordinaire, who participated in both podcasts and read early drafts of this work (and still managed somehow, despite that, to encourage us to continue the journey). Also, David Hale Smith (who got the ball rolling), Jonathan Santlofer (who kept it rolling, with a vengeance),

Duane Swierczynski (who dared to be among our first guests and to connect us to many author friends), Donna Bagdasarian, Mack Lundy, Micki McGee, Elaina Richardson, Eddie Muller, Allan Guthrie, Ken Bruen, P. J. Parrish, Scott Phillips, Reed Farrel Coleman, Rian Johnson, Lou Boxer, David Corbett, Christa Faust, Seth Harwood, Charles Ardai, Jason Starr, David Fulmer, Mike White, and Howard Rodman (among others).

We want to thank all those who have spoken with us or shared their thoughts about this project, including Mark Williams, Robert Ray, James Naremore, and the anonymous readers from UPNE. Their questions, insights, and suggestions helped make this a stronger book. Furthermore, this book is as much about the Oulipo as it is about film noir, and we must thank Warren Motte and Harry Mathews for their efforts to expand awareness about the Oulipo. We hope many who read our book will be stimulated to find out more about this group of writers and their virtuosic works.

And, of course, every road has a beginning; none of this would be possible without our families. We want to thank our parents, Monte Clute and Bonny McNerney, and Susan and Bernard Edwards, as well as our many family members who have been supportive of our podcasting and writing, especially Celia and Gary Parrott, Jim Mitchell, Chuck Mitchell, Mitchell Clute, Bernie Edwards, and Robert Edwards.

Thanks to everyone at UPNE/Dartmouth, beginning with acquiring editor Richard Pult, who has helped us immensely in bringing this project to fruition. Also, we appreciate the insight and support of the series editors Mark Williams and Adrian Randolph, advisor board members Derrick Cartwright, Mary Desjardins, Richard Dyer, Ursula Anna Fohne, and Nicholas Mirzoeff. Thanks also to our designer April Leidig-Higgins, and the staff at UPNE.

Finally, a special thank you to our podcast audience, without whom we would never have achieved such insights into noir, nor built such a vast worldwide noir community.

Preface

FILM NOIR HAS LONG been a topic of lively debate in academic and fan communities. More than a style or genre, "noir" designates a glorious and amorphous body of movies that continues to win converts and generate new discussions. While these discussions—whether print, spoken word, or new media—have generated many great insights into the films, which we will briefly outline, their terms and modes now show signs of travelling a few well-worn paths that circumscribe our understanding of noir rather than advancing it. *The Maltese Touch of Evil* charts a different course, returning to the careful study of the films themselves not to find proofs of the things we already know (or believe we know) about noir but in order to create rigorously structured and systematic wonder, from which may come new information. To signpost this new direction, we must begin our study of film noir with a discussion of an uncommon French word that helps us to consider the potential of a new approach.

Though rarely used in modern French, "the word *ouvroir* has three principal meanings: it denotes the room in a convent where the nuns assemble to work, a charitable institution where indigent women engage in needlework, and a 'sewing circle' where well-to-do ladies make clothes for the poor and vestments for the Church."[1] These meanings of *ouvroir* appealed to a collegial group of writers and mathematicians associated with the Collège de 'Pataphysique (College of Pataphysics) and interested in the works of Alfred Jarry, who initially dubbed themselves the SLE, or Séminaire de littérature expérimentale (Seminary of Experimental Literature). This group, with over fifty years of continuous activities and counting, fashioned a new name for themselves in December 1960: *ouvroir* became a major part of their new identity as they adopted the moniker Oulipo, an acronym for Ouvroir de Littérature Potentielle (Workshop of Potential Literature). As founding member, Jean Lescure recalls, "Ouvroir appealed to the modest taste we had for beautifully crafted work and good works: out of respect for morals and fine arts, we consented to join to the li the ou" (1973, 30; translation ours).[2]

In this and many subsequent statements of the group's purpose, Oulipians have insisted upon the "charitable" meanings of *ouvroir,* stating explicitly, "The Oulipo's inventions and discoveries are intended for all who wish to use them" (Mathews and Brotchie 2005, 206). Taken together, the above definitions are fundamentally oulipian in that they self-consciously establish the collaborative and open, often tongue-in-cheek, and always good-humored ethos of oulipian endeavor. Small wonder that the group's early members have included many of the most overtly experimental and self-consciously (but coyly) humorous midcentury European writers, such as Raymond Queneau, François Le Lionnais, Jacques Roubaud, Georges Perec, and Italo Calvino.

In English, *ouvroir* is usually rendered as "workshop," a translation that loses several definitional threads from the original French. But even "workshop" can have wonderful and robust connotations for a particular kind of committed and passionate space of action and reflection. In academia, a conference workshop can be an open, polyvalent, lively, and contentious location for stimulating discourse on a topic. In the film industry, writers and directors can "workshop" their movie and, in so doing, bring a greater number of gifted and committed personnel (designers, cinematographers, actors, etc.) into the formative stages of the creative act.

Because we share a love of both film noir and the Oulipo, and have for some time and in various ways been engaged in their critical appreciation, we agreed to consider what it would mean to craft an oulipian approach to the study of film noir—a densely interwoven body of films that seem to have lost their ability to surprise after having been viewed for so long through certain critical lenses. We wanted a methodology that would be fundamentally collaborative, always aware of its processes and how they impact its products, and able to accommodate and generate the sorts of insights born of self-conscious humor.

In all of our noir projects, including these pages you hold before you, we have been actively engaged in creating a workshop dedicated to embroidering new noir text(ile)s. You can call it a "sewing circle," "knitting group," or even a "workroom" for film noir scholars, fans, and creative personnel, and into this group we have welcomed everyone who contributes to the critical and creative dimensions of noir. We are grateful to the noir thinkers who have already contributed to our *Out of the Past: Investigating Film Noir* podcast project, which from the beginning has aimed to "follow various threads of inquiry" in an "attempt to unravel the vast canvas of noir."[3] We have learned much about film noir and the noir phenomenon from mystery writer, noir scholar, and Film Noir Foundation president Eddie Muller; from mystery writer and film noir scholar Megan Abbott; from Cashiers du Cinemart's Mike White; from crime writer Scott Phillips; from University of Kentucky professor Jeffrey Peters; from screenwriter and USC film professor Howard Rodman; and from director and screenwriter Rian Johnson—all of whom have participated in our workshop.

In the age of the World Wide Web, this *ouvroir* has literally stitched together a global noir community—one that seems to have bridged the academic/fan divide. We have received e-mails informing us that the podcasts are finding their way into syllabi for college film courses, are helping film students to analyze and discuss film, and are inspiring numerous fans to return to the noir films they love with a more critical eye. While we find such feedback gratifying, we are prouder still that the noir research and discussions continue online, with postings and new information from individuals who have listened to *Out of the Past.* Their valuable contributions have been an integral part of our investigations. Our hope is that critics, theorists, historians, fans, writers, and filmmakers will appreciate this approach to the analysis of film noir that does not seek to be exclusionary, nor forget that the power of film noir comes first and foremost from the movies themselves. Let's call it an *Ouvroir de Film Noir Potentiel,* or in short, an Oufinopo (Workshop of Potential Film Noir).

The first four chapters of this book lay out our method for achieving a meaningful and productive Oufinopo and consider how that method is inspired by, but differs from, other methods for reading and generating noir texts. These sections are born of our academic training, yet establish why we want to work against certain aspects of that training. Sustained consideration of the means and motivations of our reading practices helps us to understand that we are victims of our training—all of us, whether we're trained as fans or critics, filmmakers or theorists. Chapter 5, the preponderance of this book, focuses on the film noir images, scripts, and sounds that inspired us to such a degree that we felt compelled to undertake their study. Thus, our arguments about these films are born largely of the films. We try to make explicit what these films already implicitly suggest about their viewing. So it is that addressing questions of reading helps us to understand how we view the films, and viewing the films leads us back to questions of how we read.

We recognize that potential readers of this book are likely to be divided into two primary camps of experts: fans and academics (and academics themselves tend to be divided into at least two camps, as discussed in the introductory chapters). By way of analogy, we could say that, while these two groups watch the same films noir, they sit on opposite sides of the aisle and find it difficult to get together for shared inquiry; enthusiasts and scholars often share common concerns but speak in increasingly divergent idioms. While engagement with film noir strengthens bonds within each group respectively, these groups too often treat one another with suspicion and even hostility. The exchange of films noir among aficionados creates a sense of shared community—a community that often willfully ignores the bountiful insights of film and literary scholars. Scholars' engagement with theory likewise creates community but leaves many cinephiles to wonder if doctoral training intentionally teaches academics to ignore the abundant pleasures that should come from watching these films. We hope this book will get people to talk across the aisle—or at very least to exchange notes in the dark.

We recognize that, due to training and natural inclination, some readers will want to jump directly to chapter 5, filled with iconic noir images and associated commentary. Others will almost certainly want to begin with the first chapter, delving into the academic foundations of the project. We hope both types of readers will resist the urge to jump about and will instead read the entire book. One can enter the conversation at any point—indeed, the very structure of this text is intended to demonstrate that fact—but all will understand one another (and themselves as readers) better if they read the parts they're inclined to skip.

1

A Void in Film Noir Studies

What is completely strange in discourse on *film noir* is that the more elements of definition are advanced, the more objections and counter-examples are raised, the more precision is desired, the fuzzier the results become; the closer the object is approached, the more diluted it becomes. The result is that the energy deployed passes entirely into refuting or circumventing objections and not into searching for a more solid foundation. The cause of this situation seems to me to be a triple lack, historical, aesthetic, and theoretical.—Marc Vernet, *"Film Noir* on the Edge of Doom"

In order to see the subject of *film noir* as it is, one need look no farther than the films. Vernet's revisionism is like any of the neo-Freudian, semiological, historical, structural, socio-cultural, and/or auteurist assaults of the past. Film noir has resisted them all. . . . Certainly there is justification in James Damico's lament in "Film Noir: A Modest Proposal" that an "order of breezy assumptions seems to have afflicted film noir criticism from its beginnings." Unfortunately, in this latter context, a reactionary commentator like Vernet offers nothing new but just another brand of breezy assumptions. Actually, he offers a void, a *noir* hole where there once was a body of films.
—Alain Silver, "Introduction," *Film Noir Reader*

ALAIN SILVER'S critical remark that Marc Vernet creates "a void, a *noir* hole," in the corpus of film noir via his "brand of breezy assumptions" establishes two contrasting visions of the noir critic. On the one hand, there are critics of noir like Vernet, who deploy film and critical theory in their investigations and, in so doing, kill the object they are examining by turning the noir films themselves into abstract proofs of theoretical constructs (making a living body into a cadaver by dissecting its vital organs). On the other hand, there are critics of noir like Silver, text-based critics who seek to avoid overarching grand theories and return to the films themselves, commonly addressing the visual techniques and narrative structures of the noir style—or so Silver would have us believe.

What Silver does not state is that critics of his camp also make breezy assumptions. For to date, their call to look "no further than the films" has led to a corollary activity: they are the canonizers, who breezily determine what *is* and what *is not* noir—a perhaps greater violence to this corpus of film work. In these competing models of noir scholarship, there is one important similarity: the critic is a central mediating figure, an interpretive force between film and viewer, regardless of the extent to which he returns to the films.

In a prolepsis of Silver's critique, Vernet anticipates one of the problems facing critics who insist on a return to the films themselves, when he asks (parenthetically), "(Who has seen and studied all the films listed by Silver and Ward, Foster Hirsch or Robert Ottson?)" (1993, 2). Vernet is calling attention to the fact that the lists of film noir titles compiled by proponent's of Silver's approach now routinely run into the hundreds and even thousands, and such a cinematic undertaking would be a daunting task for even the most committed critic. Putting aside for the moment that there are cinephiles and film scholars who could likely answer Vernet's parenthetical in the affirmative, his question is ultimately rhetorical, since viewing all of the films noir in existence is beside the point of his essay. In reality, Vernet's concern in this 1993 essay is to redress what he perceives as a "triple lack": historical, aesthetic, and theoretical voids in film noir studies that he believes have led us down false paths of looking for points of origin, deciding on stylistic grounds what's in and what's out, and penning scholarship that depends largely on lists (of titles, of characteristics, etc.). His answer is to fill the voids in our noir investigations with a more rigorous historical, critical, and theoretical apparatus, while Silver's answer is to plug the "*noir* hole" with the films themselves.

Frank Krutnik sees this problem of diametrically opposed noir critical camps as evidence of the co-optation of noir (as an intellectual commodity) by divergent scholarly agendas: "The academic 'film community' (especially in the United States) is marked by a division, at times radical, between opposing camps of 'theorists' and 'historians.' Noir can be 'press-ganged' into the service of either faction. This intensifies its attraction, yet it also exacerbates the very problems marking both film noir itself and the current state of 'film studies'" (1991, ix).[1] As Krutnik continues his explication of the problems facing film noir studies, he reveals yet another potential "void," not only a polarization between theorists and historians within the academy but also a gap perceived by fans and some scholars between the clinical precision of academic treatments of the subject and the abundant pleasures that should come from watching films noir. In response to the common lament from the fan community—which might best be summarized by the question "Do these scholars even watch the films?"—Krutnik suggests, rather hopefully, that "the history of *noir* and pleasure in *noir* (whether from the perspective of the *aficionado* or the theorist) need not necessarily be incompatible bedfellows" (1991, 28).

We concur with Krutnik's summary and want to offer a method that reunites history, theory, and viewing pleasure. In the current state of noir studies, the critical binds identified above are unavoidable, not only because the entrenchment of oppositional critical camps has created a situation where the various sides seem constrained to establish their position in terms of the others, but more importantly because film noir is among the most self-conscious styles in film history and has itself anticipated the very critical approaches that have come to surround it. As Foster Hirsch puts it, *"Noir's visual style is as highly inflected and as self-conscious as its storytelling methods"* (1981, 78). We would suggest that noir criticism must be alert to these distinctive self-conscious inflections, for through such inflections films noir demonstrate ways in which they want to be read.

Thus, this text aims to introduce a new approach to the study of film noir that avoids the holes and double binds created by the pervading methodologies. Our working method deduces the critical paradigms inherent in the texts (born of noir's particular self-consciousness) and investigates the critical and creative potentials of these paradigms through the use of formal constraints.

This approach grows from our understanding and appreciation of the spirit and works of the Oulipo.[2] As founder, François Le Lionnais states in the group's first manifesto,

> Every literary work builds upon an inspiration (at least that is what its author lets on) that is expected to adapt itself, for better or for worse, to a series of constraints and procedures that stack inside one another like Russian nesting dolls. . . . Must humanity sit back and be satisfied with making classical verse with new thoughts? We do not believe so. What some writers have introduced in their manner, with talent (indeed, with genius) but certain ones periodically (forging new words), others with predilection (counterrhymes), others with insistence but in only one direction (Lettrism), the Workshop of Potential Literature (Oulipo) intends to do systematically and scientifically, and when necessary by resorting to a helping hand from data processing machines.[3] (1973, 20–21; translation ours)

To this end, the Oulipo undertakes two branches of activity: analysis and synthesis. The "synthetic tendency," or *synoulipism,* is concerned with "invention rather than discovery," and its primary function is to create formal constraints intended to stimulate writing. Synoulipism frequently intersects with the Oulipo's interest in mathematics as a method for generating new possibilities for exploration and discovery, and their use of computers to aid in such exploration. The "analytical tendency," or *anoulipism,* takes an ironic stance, identifying works from the past that were written under systematic constraint (such as lipograms or palindromes) and dubbing them acts of "plagiarism by anticipation" of later oulipian activity. Through anoulipism, the Oulipo claims to "y rechercher des possibilités qui dépassent souvent ce que les auteurs avaient soupçonné" ("to find there [i.e., in these works] possibilities that often exceed that which their authors had anticipated") (Le Lionnais 1973, 21; translation ours).

This simple claim belies the complexity of anoulipism in many ways. First, there is a rich ambiguity to the phrase "y rechercher." It can mean "to rediscover there," "to attempt to find there," or "to research there." Thus, anoulipism can be distinguished from most scholarly endeavor in that it is not only, or even primarily, about the *interpretation* of past works to reveal something new; rather, it *finds,* or refinds, extant aspects of those works. In this sense, Le Lionnais's statement credits the author with a certain anticipatory knowledge, while simultaneously claiming that anoulipism finds additional possibilities—what we might rightly consider potentials already buried in the original work, waiting only to be dusted off by the activity of anoulipism. We shall return to this concept in greater detail as we reexamine the pitfalls of the methodologies traditionally deployed in the study of noir, and consider how we might sidestep them using anoulipistic and synoulipistic logics to reveal the self-consciousness and constraint at the heart of films noir.[4]

One of the major oulipian works that has inspired our methodology is Georges Perec's novel *La disparition,* translated into English as *A Void.*[5] The novel is a dazzling mystery written under the lipogrammatical constraint of never using the letter *e.*[6] As characters search for the truth of what is causing their demise, they deduce it is some transcendent knowledge, unachievable in the material world of the living, and they perish at the very moment they intuit a form like the absent letter *e.*

Traditionally, scholarly glosses of *A Void*—and indeed of most oulipian texts—either frame the oulipian writer as a whimsical "producer" of literature (because author or auteur would imply too much creative genius and intentionality) or else take oulipian works too literally at their word (and thus too seriously)—as is evident in the many critical readings of *A Void* that see the lipogram *only* as a formal device that allows Perec to explore the traumatic erasures and absences born of World War II.[7]

It is undoubtedly true that formal elision is an apt narrative mechanism for suggesting and even exploring trauma. This is true in *La disparition* as well as in films noir, which often circle all around the traumatic event that set the action in motion, without having to face that event head on.[8] That midcentury film and literature should have this in common is no surprise. To quote Raymond Chandler, "We have that kind of world. Two wars gave it to us and we are going to keep it" (1995, 432).[9] However, by reading formal narrative elision *only* as the proof of traumatic historical elisions, these studies err in the other direction from those that dismiss oulipian constraints as a gimmick.

Instead of narrowing our focus on the constraint until it appears a simple game, or broadening our focus until we see in the constraint only historical referents beyond the text, we must find a way to visualize the complex interplay of constraint and diegesis in oulipian texts and films noir.[10] As we shall see, this interplay gives proof to the fact that works written under constraint are auto-exegetical in the extreme.[11]

These auto-exegetical qualities are often most visible in the humor of oulipian and noir texts, and yet it is humor that historical studies in the vein discussed above are least likely to address (or most likely to see *only* as dark, existential humor—a bitter laugh in the face of suffering).[12] We will return to a close reading of *A Void* to show not only how it embodies the oulipian concepts of "plagiarism by anticipation," "constraint," and "potential" but also how it utilizes particularly self-conscious punning language and intertextual references to other works of fiction that foreground the act of reading to structure extradiegetic spaces from which it is able to script auto-exegesis.[13]

We will then demonstrate how the calculated, playful, generative procedures that created *A Void* can be used to address a void in noir scholarship and thereby propose ways of avoiding certain reductionist tendencies and critical paralyses in existing studies of film noir.

For noir is similarly attentive in its diegetic action to the constraints of its production, and self-reflexive humor is foremost among those constraints. Despite its reputation as the "darkest" of film styles, noir is marked by a playfulness as profound and as critically charged as that in any oulipian text, as Foster Hirsch has noted:

> Bizarre backgrounds encourage the splashy visual set pieces that decorate the genre. Usually involving a chase, a murder, a showdown, a release of tension or violence, a moment of madness, the *noir* set piece is a showcase for the kind of baroque sensibility that most American genres have little use for. Defined by its bravura scale, these visual high points have a delirious humor, as if the film-makers are slyly ribbing themselves as well as the audience. (1981, 86)

In short, noir studies must be alert to the critical implications of noir's formal play. We want to offer an approach to the study of film noir that opens up the critical and creative *potential* of noir already in evidence in noir's self-consciousness.

To achieve this focus, we must momentarily turn a blind eye to many scholarly tendencies (in addition to those discussed above). For one, we are not seeking to create a comprehensive historical analysis of the development of noir as a concept. Scholarly works such as Sheri Chinen Biesen's *Blackout: World War II and the Origins of Film Noir;* Foster Hirsch's *The Dark Side of the Screen: Film Noir;* Frank Krutnik's *In a Lonely Place: Film Noir, Genre, Masculinity;* James Naremore's *More than Night: Film Noir in Its Contexts;* or Marc Bould's *Film Noir: From Berlin to Sin City* are essential readings for those interested in the history and development of film noir in this sense. And Alain Silver and James Ursini do an excellent job bringing together seminal articles, interviews, and case studies in their multivolume *Film Noir Reader* series.

Nor are we engaging with the major grand theories and theoretical paradigms circulating in noir studies. Films noir have drawn the attention of many renowned theorists, including Fredric Jameson, Noel Burch, Slavoj Zizek, Elizabeth Cowie, E. Ann Kaplan, Mary Ann Doane, and Laura Mulvey. The predominant theories of modernity, postmodernity, psychoanalysis, and feminism, to cite only a few, have been expanded and deepened by their meaningful and sustained engagement with film noir.

Further, you will not find a comprehensive definition of noir in our book or any attempt to settle long-standing debates on the precise nature of noir as a style, genre, mood, movement, cycle, idea, or phenomenon. We believe that "noir," whether it is used as an adjectival modifier of a cinematic term or as a generic noun, transgresses every attempt to assign it a conclusive definition and deftly avoids the final reckoning of even the most conscientious canonizer.

Instead, we want to show that the viewer alert to the oulipian concepts of plagiarism by anticipation, constraint, and potential—and the particular self-conscious playfulness born of these—will see that the films themselves open up new modes of inquiry: modes that generate unanticipated information; modes that impact how we study films noir and how we might create new noir texts in various media in the new millennium.

As it so happens, we examine thirty-one films noir in this study. This is no magic number, and our sample set is not meant to suggest a canon. As any fan-scholar can appreciate, we started with films we love and could enjoy watching numerous times. Some would be on anyone's list of the "most" noir films; some are less immediately recognizable as noir in their style, subject matter, or date of production.

But there is a constraint governing why we selected these particular thirty-one films: they were among the first films we discussed in our podcast series *Out of the Past: Investigating Film Noir* that was a major impetus behind this book.[14] An ongoing example of digital humanities scholarship, every episode of that project investigates a single film in relation to the body of film noir. As we were producing new episodes of that series and making film choices, we engaged with our listeners for suggestions as to which films to investigate. In retrospect, it is hard to say which films were picked due to fan interest in a particular movie and which choices were solely ours, but we appreciate that a larger (sewing) circle helped determine the form of the project from the outset.[15]

Furthermore, our choices consciously represent a diverse sampling of films. We sought to include early noir films and recently produced movies, to situate "classic" titles alongside lesser-known or marginalized films noir. In other words, these films were selected to present a polyvalent sampling of the multiple threads of film noir. Many great films noir are absent (such as *Gilda, In a Lonely Place,* and *The Big Combo*), and other films we include do not commonly appear in film noir lists (such as *It's a Wonderful Life*). We tackle major studio films (MGM's *The Postman Always Rings Twice,* Paramount's *Sunset Blvd.,* Twentieth Century Fox's *Laura,* and Warner Bros.' *The Big Sleep*), as well as B films and poverty-row fare (such as Producers Releasing Corporation's [PRC] *Detour* and Eagle-Lion Films' *He Walked by Night*). We include neo-noir movies made after the 1960s (such as *Chinatown* and *The Grifters*), revisionist hybrid noir films (such as *The Big Lebowski*), and futuristic tech noir (such as *Blade Runner* and *Batman Begins*). Finally, we add films made outside the Hollywood system (such as Jules Dassin's French film *Du rififi chez les hommes*).

To some, our choices may seem a bit eclectic, but that is part of our larger point. We are not seeking a singular, canonical definition of noir. We are seeking to expand approaches to noir studies or, rather, to show how, through careful viewing, we can come to appreciate that the films themselves expand such approaches. We want to be investigators of a phenomenon that finds itself in different kinds of movies in different periods of time across different cinematic traditions, and we believe these thirty-one films—stretched between the early forties and the first decade of the new millennium—suffice to reveal something of the vast and ever-expanding canvas of noir.

It is important to note that this selection of films is intended only as a starting point. We hope others will add their own personal favorites as they playfully investigate noir and our method for investigating noir. This project can ultimately be likened to an active user-generated electronic database destined to further enrich understanding as it grows.[16] We recognize that other scholars, fans, or filmmakers would select different films to enter into the initial "database" under consideration and different moments from within these films (moments perhaps with clearer connections to traditional notions of noir iconography).[17] That is as it should be in any approach that supports open, polyvalent, democratic inquiry into a popular film phenomenon.

Finally, we should briefly say a few words about the title of our book: *The Maltese Touch of Evil*. It is a conflation of two films traditionally seen as the bookends of the classic era of Hollywood noir: *The Maltese Falcon* (1941) and *Touch of Evil* (1958). The title is something of a provocation—a challenge to existing orthodoxies of noir historiography. It evinces a recombinant logic in keeping with oulipian practices (as we shall see) and thereby makes us alert to the self-conscious and intertextual qualities at the heart of oulipian literary, and noir filmic, production. With our eye on the playful and oulipian, rather than the deadly serious and canonical, we are more apt to see any selection to the canon as problematic, as all texts carry within them stories we critics tend to excise for the sake of cleanliness. In point of fact, *The Maltese Falcon* was the third cinematic adaptation of Dashiell Hammett's novel, and *Touch of Evil* was reedited by its studio and dumped into theaters as a B movie, sharing the marquee with Hedy Lamarr's *The Female Animal*. There are no clean beginning or end points, and there is no such thing as a sacrosanct text. Whether *The Maltese Falcon* and *Touch of Evil* are canonical texts, or are the start and end points of noir, is beside the point. In our provocative shorthand, they simply represent all of the films to which we need to return, again and again, to experience and to investigate the enduring power of film noir.

One Hundred Thousand Billion Films Noir

Oulipian Works and Potential

Although the films labeled "noir" appear to belong together, many of the explanations for their generic unity have been insufficient. . . . I shall not be seeking to claim that film noir represents exclusively a genre, or a generic subsystem or periodic transformation of the crime film, or a film movement, or a specific period of film history. Rather it seems more useful to acknowledge that *none of these critical positions exhausts the potential of noir.*—Frank Krutnik, *In a Lonely Place: Film Noir, Genre, Masculinity* (emphasis ours)

On peut admettre, sans tenter pour l'instant d'approfondir, qu'une oeuvre potentielle est une oeuvre qui ne se limite pas à ses apparences, qui contient des richesses secrètes, qui se prête volontiers à l'exploration.

(We can allow, without trying for the moment to elaborate any further, that a potential work is a work that does not limit itself to its appearances, that contains secret riches, that lends itself willingly to exploration.) (Translation ours)
—Jacques Bens, "Queneau Oulipian"

AT THE CONCLUSION of World War II, German forces withdrew from France, and with them went the embargo on Hollywood films. Quite suddenly in 1946, the French were exposed to wartime American cinema, and among its productions were a handful of films unusually dark in their themes and their mise-en-scène, prompting French film critic Nino Frank to coin the term "film noir." Among these films were John Huston's *The Maltese Falcon,* Otto Preminger's *Laura,* Edward Dmytryk's *Murder, My Sweet,* and Billy Wilder's *Double Indemnity.* Frank, in an article entitled "Un nouveau genre 'policier:' L'aventure criminelle," ("A New Kind of Police Genre: The Criminal Adventure"), observed that "these 'noir' films no longer have any common ground with run-of-the-mill police dramas" ([1946] 2003, 18; translation by Alain Silver).

Following in Frank's footsteps, several French critics would note an emerging, dark cinematic trend emanating from a new generation of Hollywood filmmakers,[1] and would group these hitherto unrelated films as *noir.*[2] In 1955, Raymond Borde and Étienne Chaumeton published their seminal book *A Panorama of American Film Noir 1941–1953.* Under the category of "film noir," Borde and Chaumeton expanded the list of noir movies to twenty-two titles, including what many consider to be the quintessential noir, Jacques Tourneur's 1947 film *Out of the Past.*[3] For fans and scholars alike, this became the foundational set of films noir from which the characteristics of noir style, narrative design, psychology, and themes were deduced.[4]

While such A restricted pool of titles had the advantage of highlighting certain core characteristics, it was also bound to whittle away at the seductive amplitude of noir, and fans and scholars alike have alternately embraced and resisted the terms and scope of Borde and Chaumeton's thesis as they've wrestled to understand and define noir's basic traits.[5] James Naremore has concluded that "there is in fact no completely satisfactory way to organize the category; and despite scores of books and essays that have been written about it, nobody is sure whether the films in question constitute a period, a genre, a cycle, a style, or simply a 'phenomenon'" (2008, 9).

In penning their study, Borde and Chaumeton were likely guided by their French academic training, which has a long and often very useful tradition of defining a problem by creating lists—an approach so ingrained in the intellectual tradition that it was already the subject of mockery for François Rabelais.[6] However, any delimitation is, to others passionate about a subject, a *de facto* violence: every canon is something of a smoking gun. By planting a flag in this field of study they called noir, Borde and Chaumeton, perhaps unwittingly, marked a rallying point around which subsequent scholarly battles would rage.

Since 1955, scholars and fans have developed numerous lists, encyclopedias, folksonomies, and filmographies of noir—all of them, it seems, motivated by an interest in making certain claims. Along with Frank Krutnik, Richard Martin has argued that noir has been intentionally co-opted by different academic factions and ideological agendas since the 1950s, thereby "becoming many things to many people" (1997, 2–3). Motivation aside, the construction of noir filmographies has involved defining sets of inclusive and exclusive characteristics, then identifying all the films that match the stated criteria—the whole process executed with what might reasonably be called mathematical logic and precision.

For example, Stephen Neale has calculated that the twenty-two films Borde and Chaumeton listed under the rubric "film noir" represent only 0.41 percent of Hollywood's total film output during the time period they studied (2000, 146).[7] Comparatively, Alain Silver and Elizabeth Ward's *Film Noir: An Encyclopedic Reference to the American Style* (1992) provides synopses of 312 films noir produced between 1941 and 1958, a more than ten-fold increase over *Panorama*'s index of titles. In a useful overview of noir filmographies, Marc Bould has cross-tallied numerous lists, starting with Paul Duncan, who identifies 1,028 films noir.[8] Then Bould adds to Duncan's list: Foster Hirsch's work adds forty-seven American neo-noir films, Robin Buss's contributes seventy-nine French films noir, and Andrew Spicer's list includes almost two hundred titles not mentioned by these other authors, including 104 British noirs (Bould 2005, 3–4). When all of the tabulations are completed, Bould's final count stands at 1,354 films. Separately, Michael F. Keaney's *Film Noir Guide* offers up 745 classic films noir from the period 1940 to 1959, with the added note that he "viewed each of the . . . films and . . . enjoyed the experience tremendously" (2003, 7).[9] And the above lists are far from exhaustive. Given such proliferation, many film noir lists are more quixotic than taxonomic.

One online noir fan named Sidney has undertaken a systematic attempt at creating a comprehensive noir filmography. His "Complete Film Noir List" creates a collated "master list" from ten and a half published noir filmographies.[10] Sidney started his list by doing a search for "film-noir" titles in the Internet Movie Database (IMDb), which yielded 437 titles.[11] To that initial group, he added titles from Silver and Ward's *Film Noir Encyclopedia;* Nicholas Christopher's *Somewhere in the Night;* Spencer Selby's *Dark City;* Michael Stephen's *Film Noir: A Comprehensive, Illustrated Reference;* Arthur Lyons's *Death on the Cheap: The Lost B Movies of Film Noir;* Keaney's *Film Noir Guide* and *British Film Noir Guide;* Duncan's *Film Noir: Films of Trust and Betrayal;* Jon Tuska's *Dark Cinema: American Film Noir;* and last but not least, Borde and Chaumeton's *Panorama of American Film Noir.* The resultant list has 1,192 films noir. Prompted by a friend who complained about the number of titles, Sidney then cross-referenced the "complete" list for "consensus" picks that showed up on at least seven of the ten lists he consulted and published his "Consensus Film Noir List." That smaller list, which constitutes something akin to a scholarly consensus, contains 293 films made between 1940 and 1959.

In describing his efforts to create "complete" and "consensus" film noir lists, Sidney has shared with the public his correspondence with a DVD producer who wrote him with a word of warning:

I'd caution you not to put too much faith in the film noir guides, since it's not as if there's some Film Noir Licensing Board that reviews films and hands out Certificates of Authenticity. The authors of those books are just people, limited by their own knowledge of and access to films for review, so guidebooks on noir are naturally weighted towards the more readily available studio pictures, like *Double Indemnity* or *Kiss Me Deadly* or *The Big Sleep,* since the many low-budget B noirs from indie producers or overseas have mostly fallen into obscurity.[12]

This is a powerful reminder of the problems that arise as one tries to assemble comprehensive lists. Beyond the difficulties of selecting and tabulating, there is the greater problem that many films noir (who knows how many) are inaccessible, decomposing, lost, or simply forgotten. And while concerned critics, preservationists, and foundations race to locate and save noir films in archival danger, there are likely many that will never be saved in time.

This story also reminds us that, in days to come, noir lists may be generated based on accessibility rather than artistry, and may favor industrial logics and contemporary marketing schemes over scholarly categorizations. Consider how businesses such as Netflix, Blockbuster, Amazon, and Wal-Mart categorize and arrange their DVDs and movie rentals using computer databases that allow films to be tagged with metadata such as genre, year of release, production personnel, and user-generated keywords. Whether deserved or not, the designation "noir" can potentially enhance a film's rental or sales status. Furthermore, a company like Netflix uses a complex, mathematically calculated recommendation system to evaluate rental patterns and make suggestions to its members.[13] Such corporate strategies impact the marketplace and do much to elevate or deflate a film noir's status and accessibility to the general public, independent of the film's stature in fan and scholarly communities.

A quick search of "film noir" in the Netflix database brings up a list of its most frequently rented noir titles (a list that is additionally constrained by the titles' availability in DVD format in the United States). It is an admixture and on any given day is likely to include star vehicles like *The Big Sleep,* lesser-known titles like *The Scavengers,* and noirs *en couleur* such as *Leave Her to Heaven.* In many ways, the ever-changing rental lists at online sites such as Netflix are another type of potential noir filmography, built from recombinant, user-generated patterns.

By these standards, the potential number of films noir is somewhere between a few dozen and more than a thousand. And if one agrees that films noir are still being produced in the twenty-first century and need not be American, then any list will continue to expand.[14] As Naremore states, "One thing is clear: the last film noir is no easier to name than the first" (2008, 39).

In short, it is an understatement to say there is no fundamental agreement as to the basic criteria for defining "film noir." Furthermore, these issues around "explanations, interpretations and definitions of noir" point to a deeper methodological concern, as Neale has so aptly noted:

> The problem—or at least the problem with *noir*'s proponents—is that the systematic application of many of the criteria they have advanced as definitive tend either to necessitate the exclusion or marginalization of films and genres generally considered as central, or else to necessitate the inclusion of films and genres generally considered as marginal. This in turn has knock-on effects for those who ascribe a socio-historical significance to *noir,* or who wish to explain and interpret its ideological features and functions. (2000, 144)

This is a central problem subtending critical approaches to film noir that we seek to redress in this book. For attempting to define and understand film noir through inclusionary or exclusionary logics "inevitably generates contradictions, exceptions, and anomalies, and is doomed, in the end, to incoherence" (Naremore 2008, 145). Such approaches enervate not only noir scholarship but even noir filmmaking: they sap the critical *and* the creative by producing reductive, generic, and constrictive characteristics that work to delimit the creativity of the past and forestall or foreclose the artistic possibilities of the future.

Yet it is easy to understand the appeal of such approaches, for numbers and sets (falsely) promise objectivity and quantitative cleanliness. The numbers are not at fault but rather the impulses driving critics to do the math.

But numbers and sets also open the door to methodologies far richer and more entertaining—to wit, the vast potential of recombinant poetics.

The Oulipo saw mathematics as a way to invent, stimulate, rediscover, and analyze literature. As François Le Lionnais states in the first manifesto, "Mathematics—particularly the abstract structures of contemporary mathematics—propose a thousand directions for exploration, taking as a point of departure Algebra (recourse to new laws of composition) as much as Topology (considerations of proximity, opening or closure of texts)" (1973, 21; translation ours).[15] Thus, the Oulipo saw its activities and mission as "rais[ing] the problem of the efficacy and the viability of artificial (and, more generally, artistic) literary structures" (Le Lionnais 1986, 30).

With such oulipian activities in mind, we will not try to quantify how many films noir there are but rather use a different kind of mathematical logic to ask, "How many *potential* films noir are there?" For this leads us to the more important corollary, "What is the *potential* of film noir?"

Potential is a key concept in oulipian work, for it is the *po* that was consensually added to the *ou* and the *li*. Harry Mathews puts it in these terms:

> The last word of *Ouvroir de littérature potentielle* defines the specificity of the Oulipo. From its beginnings the group has insisted on the distinction between "created creations" (créations créées) and "creations that create" (créations créé- antes), to the benefit of the latter: it has been concerned not with literary works but with procedures and structures capable of producing them. When the first sonnet was written almost a thousand years ago, what counted most was not the poem itself but a new potentiality of future poems. Such potentialities are what the Oulipo invents or discovers. (Mathews and Brotchie 2005, 213)

For an apt introduction to this concept of potential (in the oulipian sense), let us turn to mathematician and writer Raymond Queneau's poetry collection *Cent mille milliards de poèmes* (*One Hundred Thousand Billion Poems*).[16] It consists of ten sonnets, each written in the same rhyme scheme such that any verse might be substituted for any other in each of the ten poems. Thus, the total number of poems that might be generated from these ten (each fourteen verses long) is 10^{14}, or one hundred trillion (100,000,000,000,000). The potential of such a work, the total number of texts it represents, could never be exhausted by any reader. In fact, it represents far more words than have been written in the history of the world. We see that the potential inherent in this poem calls attention to what might best be called *recombinatorial* poetics, where the form itself forces us repeatedly to consider the implications of the form.[17]

Cent mille milliards de poèmes has an important place in the history and development of the Oulipo. As Bens states,

> It is necessary to remark, yet again, that it was unjust to consider Queneau's combinatorial poems as "the first work of potential literature," for potential literature existed before the foundation of the Oulipo (that is, in fact, what we're trying to demonstrate here). On the other hand, what one can affirm without any great risk of error is that [this work] constitutes the first *conscious* work of potential literature. Or rather: *concerted.*
>
> Yes, I prefer concerted, because Raymond Queneau does not have the reputation of letting "the unconscious" to take over his writing. (Bens 1981; translation ours)[18]

Jacques Roubaud is similarly laudatory about the impact of Queneau's text: "Its constraint is rather elementary, but its potentiality is spectacular" (2004, 100–101).[19]

Another way of comprehending potential in an oulipian sense is to define what it is not. It is not an aleatory method producing chance outcomes. It is not a surrealist method. In fact, Oulipians defined potential in distinction to the "automatism" or unconscious operations of surrealist methods and surrealist games such as "the exquisite corpse,"[20] as we can see in Roubaud's chapter "The Oulipo and Combinatorial Art":

> The limiting and at the same time crucial role of mathematics in Oulipian art represents an intentional choice on the part of its founders. Their basic reason was that, in Queneau's and Le Lionnais's view, after the exhaustion of the generative power of traditional constraints, only mathematics could offer a way

out between a nostalgic obstinacy with worn-out modes of expression and an intellectually pathetic belief in "total freedom." It was a matter, at least at the start, of asserting a theoretical anti-Surrealism. But beyond that historically dated disagreement, it was also a matter of taking a stand in the eternal and universal quarrel between advocates and opponents of "formalism," with all the subsidiary antagonisms which that implies. ([1991] 2005, 40)

This distinction between surrealist automatism and oulipian potential can be charted clearly through the career of Queneau. In his youth, Queneau was a surrealist,[21] and in 1928 he married Janine Kahn, whose sister was the wife of aurrealist André Breton. But he eventually broke from both surrealism and his brother-in-law. Marc Lowenthal summarized this change of heart in his book on Queneau:

> The Oulipo has offered the best counterargument to the automatic-writing practices of the Surrealists, encouraging writers to, in the words of Queneau, "escape that which is called inspiration." For Queneau, the typical act of inspiration draws from limited resources. Rather than restricting the possibilities of creation, he argued, the use of artificial structure—mathematical and otherwise—opens the way to the vaster range of potential creation. This "potential" was not what he saw as the limited potential of the subconscious (the arena of automatic writing), but the potential of the conscious. (2000, xii)

We would propose that, like Queneau's *Cent mille milliards de poèmes,* much of film noir lies in a *potential* state. By reading even a large sample set of films noir in their integral (i.e., "theatrical release") form, without substituting certain "verses" (shots, scenes, sequences, etc.) of noir stories with others to give them new context, we have experienced only a sliver of noir narrative. Through mathematically rigorous recombinatorial poetics, we can consciously liberate the potential of film noir.

In other words, it is time to expand our vision of potential works of noir and, more importantly, our understanding of how the potential of noir works.

3

Workshop of Potential Criticism

Anoulipism and Plagiarism by Anticipation

La lecture potentielle a le charme de faire ressortir la duplicité des textes, qu'ils soient
oulipiens ou non.

   (*Potential reading* has the charm of making manifest the duplicity of texts, be they
oulipian or not.)—Harry Mathews, "L'algorithme de Mathews'"

An algorithm is a set of rules that, applied in a prescribed order to a set of data,
produces a result, no matter what that data may be.
—François Le Lionnais, *Dictionnaire des mathématiques,* in *The Oulipo Compendium*
  (translation by Harry Mathews)

THIS BOOK PROPOSES an Oufinopo, or a Workshop of Potential Film Noir (and, more broadly, a demonstration of Oucritpo, or Workshop of Potential Criticism).[1] As the last chapter demonstrated, we seek to discover, invent, and utilize constraints to yield new noir potentialities.

One of the first tasks of the anoulipistic act of discovery is to look to the past to see what earlier studies or formal exercises might be considered "plagiarism by anticipation" of this newly formed *ouvroir*. For as the Oulipo has demonstrated, what is ostensibly created as a new constraint (synoulipism) may actually prove to have been invented in the past, only to be rediscovered through oulipian activity (anoulipism).

As we searched through the history of film noir studies, few approaches, if any, seemed to involve constraint, combinatorics, or mathematics in the oulipian sense. But as we broadened our search beyond film noir into cinema studies, we did find a novel methodology being used by Robert Ray that was motivated by some of the same desires and seemingly shared some of the same methods as our *ouvroir* of film noir.

In *The Avant-Garde Finds Andy Hardy,* Ray champions "avant-garde models for new ways of writing and thinking about the movies" (1998, 1). In articulating a critical approach to film studies based on surrealist games (automatism and aleatory methods), he aims to overcome certain impasses of film studies—largely the same impasses we've discussed above in terms of noir scholarship. Curiously, however, he does not start the book with a surrealist exercise but rather an oulipian one.

Ray's opening chapter follows the structure of Italo Calvino's brilliantly executed oulipian novel *If on a Winter's Night a Traveler.* Through numerous incipits à la *Winter's Night,* Ray is able to reflect self-consciously on the text he is in the process of creating:

> That discussion—of film studies' impasse, of the avant-garde's potential— would amount to an alternate way to start this book, one that would concern itself less with the announced subject matter ... than with the means that film scholars have developed for thinking and writing about them. (1998, 10)

Beyond sharing many of our motivations, Ray even seems to anticipate our methodology:

> Although in this book the avant-garde arts could appear as nothing more than a provocation, a satisfying slap in the face of conventional film studies, they actually provide a means for bringing film criticism into some sort of relationship with the communications technologies revolutionizing everyday life. Indeed, far from being useless, the experimental arts amount to a "workshop for potential criticism." (1998, 16)[2]

As a work of plagiarism by anticipation of our Oufinopo, we appreciate Ray's call for "improper questions" to challenge what he calls film studies' "enormously powerful theoretical machine" and his search for new methods that "both produce information (by remaining unpredictable) and respond to the new technologies (by becoming experimental)" (1998, 16). However, Ray ultimately does not (and in fact, cannot) pursue potential criticism in any truly oulipian sense. For the Oulipo (as they make quite explicit) is not an avant-garde, and the oulipian concept of potential cannot be understood through such a lens. As Ray weaves between moments of oulipian constraint and reveries of surrealist automatism—blurring many distinctions between the two—we see how different our projects really are.[3]

After exploring "the avant-garde arts as a model for different ways of writing and thinking about movies," (1998, 94) Ray turns to a discussion of Roland Barthes's 1978 lecture on Proust:

> [Barthes] had located a model in a "third form, neither Essay nor Novel," which he traced back to Proust, who had stood "at the intersection of two paths, two genres, torn between two 'ways' he does not yet know could converge." … This *third form* would not abandon criticism's knowledge effect. But it would adopt what Barthes called "the novelesque," a method of writing that would draw on fiction's resources. (Ray 1998, 95)

Ray considers how Barthes's subsequent work was inspired by this third form in ways that might reinvigorate film studies and revisits Barthes's alphabetic autobiography in order to consider how that exercise could help film scholars better address "cinema's radical break with alphabetic culture" (1998, 114).

Ray scripts two series of alphabetic studies, one focused on a vast array of critical, pop culture, and historical phenomena that seem to bear some revealing relationship to visual theory ("The ABCs of Visual Theory"), then a second focused on Andy Hardy films ("The ABCs of Andy Hardy"). While such constraint might sound oulipian, Ray frames the exercise as a surrealist attempt to discover "the advantages of yielding the initiative to a given form" (1998, 123)—a very different form of activity than struggling with formal constraint to unleash the potential of the *conscious,* as Raymond Queneau made explicit.[4]

In Ray's first series, the letter *O* is given over to a discussion of the Oulipo. After providing an apt summary of the Oulipo's origins and activities, Ray views oulipian work through the lens of historically concurrent developments in critical theory:

> With them (the Oulipo), pseudo-science became practical aesthetics, a way of getting started, a serious game without metaphysical consequences. Similarly, Derrida's puns and coincidental etymologies serve only as sifting devices, vehicles for filtering the massive wash of information for traces of possible knowl-

edge, a prospecting tool designed to locate that hidden region where two apparently discreet discourses share a common vocabulary. (1998, 134)

While Ray's inclusion of the Oulipo signposts another meaningful route to asking "improper questions" that would lead to new information, his acceptance of the common critical gloss of the Oulipo—which views the Oulipo as an avant-garde or as a literary manifestation of the critical environment critics are always (already) likely to focus upon—quickly closes that road. In one sense, this is just as well, because the Oulipo *"n'est pas une littérature aléatoire"* ("is not an aleatory literature") and is fundamentally incompatible with surrealism.[5] On the other hand, it is a road worth taking, one we believe shows how a "workshop of potential criticism" built upon oulipian practices may supply a better framework than surrealism for generating surprising film studies research.

Strangely, the proof of this contention may already be in Ray's text. In his second alphabetic series, *N* stands for "Noir and Andy Hardy." This entry allows Ray to discover that 1941's *Life Begins for Andy Hardy* is, in fact, a film noir. Ray identifies several noir tropes in the film, released in the same year as *The Maltese Falcon:* "a gritty New York rooming house, a femme fatale . . . a sudden death, and images of poverty, homelessness, and unemployment" (1998, 159). In many ways, Ray is performing a potential reading of an Andy Hardy film that reveals that film's duplicity as a text; *Life Begins for Andy Hardy* is a heartwarming family film, perhaps, but still a film that cannot escape the doom descending upon the wartime world and upon the Hollywood system producing its first films noir.[6]

It is a powerful demonstration of how film studies, and noir studies, can be advanced through potential criticism that uses rigorous constraints, such as strictly alphabetic lists. Though Ray might not agree with such an assessment, we would suggest his great noir insight into *Life Begins for Andy Hardy* is not the surprising result of an aleatory mechanism but instead the outcome of oulipian constraint and that this oulipian exercise undermines his aforementioned gloss of the Oulipo.

In other words, by framing "constraint" within a discussion of surrealism, and explicating the Oulipo through the work of poststructuralist theory

(Barthes and Derrida), Ray circumscribes the potential of oulipian potential. Rather than viewing oulipian work as a manifestation of critical theory, it is potentially more revealing to view theory as an act of plagiarism (not always by anticipation) of the great insights brought about by oulipian endeavor.

Indeed, it is difficult to read about Barthes overcoming writer's block through constraint ("to adopt the succession of letters in order to link fragments is to fall back on what constitutes the glory of language... which is not arbitrary" [Barthes 1989a, 147]) and not think about Queneau's best counterargument to surrealism, namely, that artificial restrictions allow writers to "escape that which is called inspiration." And when Ray writes, "In the world of Hollywood filmmaking in particular, the strict management of signification makes every object an index, capable of opening at a touch into stores of knowledge" (1998, 121), it is hard to not hear echoes of Georges Perec's intertextuality, "citational art,"[7] and the power of his lipogrammatic writing. Thus, while we appreciate Ray's version of a "workshop of potential criticism," we start from a fundamentally different set of assumptions about constraint, and about the Oulipo, as we form our Oucritpo.

As we have seen, the Oulipo undertakes two branches of activity: synthesis and analysis. As founding member François Le Lionnais points out, the work of synthesis (synoulipism)—the creation of new literary procedures, or new forms of literary constraint—"is the more ambitious; it constitutes the essential vocation of the Oulipo." Key to this project, and to what Oulipians consider its "scientific" rigor, is the formal logic of mathematics. For reasons made clear above, we would put equal emphasis on the analytic branch of oulipian activity, for anoulipism helps us to "find" potentials inherent in existing texts.[8] The anoulipistic discovery of acts of "plagiarism by anticipation" is also provocative in other ways; by reversing the usual trajectory of influence, it troubles the concept of *framing* reading. Which text structures the frame through which the reader reads the other? Moreover, can the reader properly read an oulipian text without reading the others that oulipian text references through its formal play and/or through overt citation?

One potentially fruitful way to delve deeper into the topics of synoulipism and anoulipism is through Oulipian Harry Mathews's constraint

"Mathews's Algorithm." Elected to the Oulipo in 1973, and a friend of Perec, Mathews created an algorithm that has many "syntactic, semantic, and analytic uses" (2005, 184).

The algorithm's operation is based on the permutation of heterogeneous elements. Typically, Mathews's algorithm is set into a 4 × 4 table of data, where most of the elements must be different from each other. So this might look like the table below, using the words film, noir, hail, and male.[9]

F	I	L	M
N	O	I	R
H	A	I	L
M	A	L	E

The next operation, the permutation, is to shift each set n-1 places to the right. This means you would leave the first row untouched, but shift the second row one place, the third row two places and so on, such that the resultant would look like the table below.

F	I	L	M
R	N	O	I
I	L	H	A
A	L	E	M

Once the shift is complete, one can see the resultant words. Reading upward from the underlined letters, we now have fair, nill,[10] hole, and maim —words with the potential to reveal new information about the sample set (and, given the nature of the sample set, about noir itself). There are many variants on this algorithm, and Mathews suggests that the user of the algorithm determine the number of lines and columns.

Mathews's algorithm can also be used on more complex elements, such as lines of poetry, or a film noir equivalent such as lines of dialogue. Another table of data might be constructed from these four spoken, hard-boiled lines from, respectively, *Double Indemnity, Out of the Past, The Asphalt Jungle,* and *Detour:*

> How could I have known that murder could sometimes smell like
>   honeysuckle?
> A dame with a rod is like a guy with a knitting needle.
> Crime is only a left-handed form of human endeavor.
> Whichever way you turn, fate sticks out a foot to trip you.

Using the algorithm's "rule of equivalence" (whereby each element of a set needs to be consistent with the corresponding elements of the other sets), these lines of dialogue need to be reduced and arranged by similarly functioning units, such as subjects, modifiers, verbs, and auxiliary words. A 4 × 4 table composed of these elements looks like this:

I	murder	(like) honeysuckle	(could have) known, (could) smell
dame (with a rod)	guy (with a knitting needle)	like	is
Crime	(human) endeavor	(left-handed) form	is
You	fate	foot (to trip you)	turns, sticks out

Performing the shift to the right, one achieves the table below.

I	murder	(like) honeysuckle	(could have) known, (could) smell
is	dame (with a rod)	guy (with a knitting needle)	like
(left-handed) form	is	crime	(human) endeavor
fate	foot (to trip you)	turns, sticks out	you

After reintroducing the auxiliary words, we can now compose four new lines of film noir dialogue, reading upward from the underlined words:

I am only a left-handed form of fate.
Whichever way a dame with a rod murders, she has a foot to trip you.
A crime turned by a guy with a knitting needle sticks out like honeysuckle.
How could you have known that you sometimes smell like human endeavor?

Mathews playfully describes some of the further applications for his algorithm:

The algorithm would be capable of processing fragments of letters—either graphic or phonetic—and the components thereof, not to mention amoebas, atoms, and quarks. It could apply itself not just to episodes of fiction, but to entire books, to entire literatures, to civilizations, to planetary and solar systems, to galaxies—in sum, to all that can be manipulated in its material or symbolic form.[11] (1988, 92; translation ours)

There is no reason, then, that shots, scenes, sequences, soundtracks, or other attributes of films noir could not be similarly permutated by a constraint such as Mathews's—a constrained undertaking that could stimulate not only the creative process of making new noir texts but more importantly for our purposes the critical process of coming to understand noir's inherent potentials.

One of the first American scholars to take interest in the Oulipo was Warren Motte, and to this day he is among the most insightful readers of oulipian work. However, his translation of Mathews's essay "L'algorithme de Mathews" exemplifies a tendency in oulipian scholarship to undervalue the ways that both anoulipism and synoulipism already enact analysis.[12]

Mathews's essay begins thus: "*La lecture potentielle* a le charme de faire ressortir la duplicité des textes, qu'ils soient oulipiens ou non" (1988, 91). A direct translation would be "*Potential reading* has the charm of making manifest the duplicity of texts, be they oulipian or not." Mathews then proceeds to run source texts through his recombinatorial algorithm (as we've seen above) and declares—if we again attempt the most direct possible translation—the following: "The resultants derived from these texts can be used to two different ends: either the 'analysis' of the texts put in play, or the creation of a new work" (1973, 105). It is crucial to note that, in the original French "can be used" is "peuvent s'utilizer," a reflexive construction that literally means "can use themselves."

Motte chooses to translate the same passages in this manner: "From the reader's point of view, the existence in literature of potentiality in its Oulipian sense has the charm of introducing duplicity into all written texts, whether Oulipian or not. . . . The results yielded by existing works can be used in two ways: either as a means of commenting on those works or as materials for inventing new ones" (1986, 126, 138).

This translation understates what oulipian texts do to read themselves and therefore may not be alert to the ways these texts plagiarize by anticipation much of the critical scholarship they inspire.[13] To say that these "results" can be used "as a means for commenting upon" the existing works is a weaker claim than to say they can use themselves in the "analysis" of the originals.

Mathews seems to suggest that oulipian procedures simultaneously generate new texts and the seeds of textual analysis—for both are "resultants" of the same constraint. In other words, producing texts under constraint is both a creative and an autoanalytical act, which explains why Mathews begins the essay with a discussion of "potential reading" and claims it makes manifest the duplicity of texts produced through oulipian constraint. It is important to note that, in this formulation, "analysis" does not necessarily require an external reader, let alone the exegetical paradigms that reader brings to the reading. Not only do Motte's translations erase the concept of potential reading, but they also focus on reception, suggesting that the "reader's point of view" is somehow necessary to "commenting upon" these texts.

We have seen critical tendencies similar to Motte's in exegeses of *A Void*, a text that problematizes those exegeses by constantly demonstrating how fully oulipian texts written under constraint read themselves. While Perec penned texts under numerous constraints generated through the activities of synoulipism, his writing was also deeply engaged in anoulipism.[14] In fact, he once described his fiction as an "art citationnel" ("citational art"), and the "Post-scriptum" of *A Void* seems to explore what that means in practical terms:

> Il comprit alors qu'à l'instar du'un Frank Lloyd Wright construisant sa maison, il façonnait mutatis mutandis, un produit prototypal qui . . . ouvrait sur un pouvoir mal connu, un pouvoir dont on avait fait fi, mais qui, pour lui, mimait, simulait, honorait la tradition qui avait fait un *Gargantua,* un *Tristram Shandy.*
>
> (He understood that, in the fashion of Frank Lloyd Wright building his home, he was creating, by making those changes that needed to be made, a prototypal product that . . . opened onto a little-known power, a power that many had disdained but that, for him, mimicked, simulated, honored the tradition that had produced a *Gargantua,* a *Tristram Shandy.*) (Perec 1969, 311; translation ours)

While Perec insists that this tradition is marked above all "par la jubilation, par l'humour biscornu" ("by jubilation, by quirky humor"), critics have tended to assume that the "text" Perec most commonly references is history.

As highlighted in our chapter 2 discussion of the critical reception of *A Void,* scholars have often and aptly noted that *e* is the only vowel needed in French to spell the words "mother" and "father" ("mère" and "père"), and Perec lost his father to the front lines and his mother to Auschwitz. But perhaps not enough has been made of the fact that by removing the *è* that makes manifest mother and father, Perec also removes the "accents graves," which might be seen both as simple markers of pronunciation and as traces of something "heavy, grave, serious, dangerous, low" (for such are the nondiacritical meanings of "grave"). In other words, the formal elision at the heart of the novel might well allow Perec to write obliquely of trauma, but if that's true then the very same elision simultaneously and self-consciously eliminates the most "heavy" and "serious" marks of traumatic absence. If we return to Perec's characterization of his citational art as part of a tradition marked by "jubilation" and "humour biscornu," we appreciate how his humor can be both serious and facetious, both reflexive and self-reflexive. For humor to see itself as jubilant, it must position itself with regard to that which it sees as serious. And for humor to know it is "biscornu"—commonly translated as "quirky" but more literally "two-horned"—it must know it's pointing in more than one direction.

Thus, we prefer to focus on oulipian process over product. Rather than suppose the "reader's point of view" is somehow necessary to "commenting upon" the formal aspects of *A Void,* we want to understand how constraints produce resultants that can be used (or "use themselves") in the analysis of the texts "put in play." In other words, we want to embrace the potential in "potential reading." In the context of *A Void*—and, for reasons chapters 4 and 5 will make clear, in the context of film noir—this requires more sustained consideration of citational art and two-horned humor.

As we have discussed at length elsewhere, there seem to be three crucial components to Perec's "citational art": *intertextual allusions* to other fictions that foreground the act and limitations of reading (most notably Edgar Allan Poe's "Purloined Letter," Henry James's "Figure in the Carpet," François Rabelais's *Quart Livre,* and Herman Melville's *Moby Dick*), which are arranged with mathematical precision in *La disparition;* the "humour biscornu" ("two-horned humor") of his novel, which we see as *self-reflexive punning* that simultaneously creates and comments upon the narrative action; and *a formal mathematical logic* that allows the text to explore, and ultimately map, its own "topology."[15] Taken together, these allow Perec to elaborate what we would call a "geometry of auto-exegesis." With this geometry, the text frames an extradiegetic (standing outside the narrative) space from which it can turn and reflect upon the diegetic (narrative) action. It literally enacts potential reading.[16]

With this understanding of oulipian *constraint* and *potential reading* in place, we would now like to examine how readings of noir have fallen into many of the same traps as readings of oulipian texts and suggest this is because critics have had a hard time in both cases recognizing or acknowledging how, through calculated intertextual borrowings and self-conscious humor, these film noir texts read themselves.

4

Build My Scaffolding High
Noir Films as Constrained Texts

Modern filmmakers are clearly unabashed in their affinity for *noir,* and
the function of self-consciousness in their work.
—Todd Erickson, "Kill Me Again: Movement Becomes Genre"

Working in an industrially defined sub-genre with as distinctive a strategy and
style as the B *film noir* imposed a number of constraints on "creativity" but . . .
such constraints should not be seen as merely negative in their operation.
—Paul Kerr, "My Name Is Joseph H. Lewis"

Art is born of constraint, lives on struggle, dies of freedom.
—André Gide, *The Evolution of the Theater*

It is necessary to create constraints, to invent freely.
—Umberto Eco, "Postscript," *The Name of the Rose*

W HILE TO SOME it may still seem strange to compare films noir to oulipian texts, there are in fact good reasons for doing so —both in terms of their modes of production and their critical reception.

Due to censorship and the conventions of genre filmmaking in classic Hollywood, films made during the studio system era had to respect certain generic tendencies and leave many things unsaid. Yet, there was the imperative to make largely similar stories fresh and marketable. To overcome these challenges, Hollywood developed a consistent set of visual tropes to imply certain narrative events: the open window with the curtains flapping stood in for lovemaking; the descent of a staircase demonstrated a character's falling fortunes; the failure to see oneself in a mirror implied a fatal lack of self-knowledge.[1]

Rather than being flattened by such conventions, these films were often enriched, the best of them demonstrating that such constraints could be a powerful, creative force for generating new texts. John O. Thompson summarizes the situation quite aptly:

On constraint: having to work within limits produces *formal* solutions with their own elegance and beauty. Wouldn't it be a bit philistine to point to the constraints of the sonnet as making it unlikely that the poet could produce satisfying work, having to keep to fourteen lines and a rhyme scheme? In media studies the outstanding example of formalist rehabilitation of elaborately constrained work has been our discovery of how very, very beautiful, whatever else they may be, the products of classic Hollywood studio system were. (1992, 296)

Read out of context, this quote is equally descriptive of oulipian poetics.[2]

While all classic Hollywood films can rightly be considered constrained texts, we would maintain that films noir were constrained in a particularly oulipian fashion, as others have intimated without explicitly framing their argument in terms of the Oulipo. Indeed, the more one reads of noir scholarship, the more one has the impression everyone has been trying to understand noir constraint in an oulipian sense, but often without the prerequisite knowledge of the Oulipo to make their positions explicit—what we might call "pure" instances of plagiarism by anticipation of our Oufinopo, for they occur without the foreknowledge necessary to true plagiary.[3]

In their chapter on noir visual style, "Some Visual Motifs of Film Noir," Janey Place and Lowell Peterson enumerate how certain stylistic qualities of noir were born of production realities but were in turn embraced for their narrative potentials; budgetary constraints and the limitations of cinema technology governed the production of noir films in the Hollywood system but led to more inventive filmmaking with its own distinctive look and stories befitting that look. As Place and Peterson explain, low-key lighting —born of low production values—combined with a desire for depth of focus to show noir protagonists in their environments resulted in the need for cinematographers to use wide-angle lenses (to compensate for low light levels) that "have certain distorting characteristics, which, as *noir* photography developed, began to be used expressively" ([1974] 1996, 67). They cite Orson Welles's first shot of Hank Quinlan in *Touch of Evil* as an example of the expressive use of such lensing that had once been pure necessity. Moreover, Place and Peterson note that expensive camera movements (such as "elaborate tracking or boom shot(s)") tended to be avoided and replaced instead by juxtapositions of extreme high-angle long shots with huge "choker" close-ups, generating "unsettling variations on the traditional close-up, medium and long shots" (67). In other words, some of the best-known examples of the noir style in the classical period resulted from both budgetary constraints and the director's willingness to embrace such constraints in an oulipian sense—to explore how they might stimulate the creative process and leave their formal traces on the diegetic action.

In his chapter "Out of What Past? Notes on B Film Noir," Paul Kerr made a similar argument, showing how constrained production values and constraints of censorship functioned together to stimulate noir storytelling:

> Artistic ingenuity in the face of economic intransigence is one critical commonplace about the B film noir (and about people like Lewton and Ulmer in particular). Against this, I have suggested that a number of noir characteristics can at least be associated with—if not directly attributed to—economic and therefore technological constraints. The paucity of "production values" (sets, stars and so forth) may even have encouraged low budget production units to compensate with complicated plots and convoluted atmosphere. Realist denotation would have thus been de-emphasized in favor of expressionist connotation. . . . This connotative quality might also owe something to the influence of the Hays Office, which meant that "unspeakable subjects could only be suggested." ([1979] 1996, 116)

In short, while initially unavoidable, these constraints were embraced by filmmakers for their creative *potentials*.[4]

Importantly, directors and cinematographers self-consciously framed their borrowings—from the reuse of existing movies sets and stock footage cited by Kerr, to the careful framing of what we might call "tribute" shots to other films noirs—in ways that called attention to the act of reusing the old material to create the new.[5] But such borrowings were not always visual. Hard-boiled literary source material could likewise be appropriated in a self-conscious fashion. One senses that part of the creative genius of John Huston's *Maltese Falcon* (1941) is that it constrained itself to Dashiell Hammett's novel to such a degree, literally transcribing crucial passages word for word and thereby creating a film masterpiece where earlier, looser adaptations had flopped. Compare, for example, this vision of the character of Sam Spade in Hammett's novel and Huston's screenplay:

Hammett

Spade, barefooted in green and white checked pajamas, sat on the side of his bed. He scowled at the telephone on the table while his hands took from beside it a packet of brown papers and a sack of Bull Durham tobacco. . . . Cold steamy air blew in through two open windows, bringing with it half a dozen times a minute the Alcatraz's foghorn's dull moaning. A tinny alarm clock, insecurely mounted on a corner of *Duke's Celebrated Criminal Cases of America*—face down on the table—held its hands at five minutes past two. (Hammett [1929] 1992, 11–12)

Huston

INT. SPADE'S ROOM

Spade, barefoot in checked pajamas, sits on the side of his bed scowling at the telephone. The hands of a tinny alarm clock, which sits on a volume of "Duke's Celebrated Criminal Cases of America," are at five minutes past two. Spade scratches the back of his neck, reaches for a packet of brown papers and a sack of tobacco by the telephone, makes a cigarette with deliberate care, licks it, puts it in his mouth. The curtains at the two open windows flutter. From across the bay comes the dull moaning of the Alcatraz fog horn. Spade sits for several moments with the cold cigarette in his mouth. Then he reaches for the telephone again, dials a number. Waiting for the answer, he shivers. (Huston [1941] 2004)

And Huston was not alone in embracing constrained adaptation in noir filmmaking. François Truffaut has discussed his adaptation of David Goodis's noir novel *Shoot the Piano Player* into his second major film (*Tirez sur le pianiste,* 1960) in these terms: "I was free as a breeze. Therefore I chose some limit so that I wouldn't go crazy. I put myself in the position of a filmmaker who had orders imposed on him: a detective novel, American, that was transposed to France" (Monaco 2004, 50).

These practices are highly analogous to oulipian intertextual borrowing, and in noir as in oulipian texts, these carefully framed appropriations result simultaneously in diegetic action and analysis of that action—just like Georges Perec's "citational art" and Harry Mathews's "potential reading." As is true of oulipian literary output, the very corpus of film noir constitutes a dense catalog of self-conscious intertextual allusions and diegetic moments that bear the formal traces of self-imposed constraint.

Perhaps the best proof that classical Hollywood filmmaking, and in particular noir filmmaking, was constrained in the oulipian sense is that, as the studio system collapsed in the postwar period, the great auteurist directors filming noir stories often took it upon themselves to impose artificial constraints to stimulate their storytelling and to explore new filmic possibilities. Consider the highly constrained, formalist experiment of Alfred Hitchcock's 1948 noir-ish film *Rope*. Hitchcock thought his crime narrative would have a greater psychological impact if he could give the impression it was one continuous shot in the long-take style. But the reels used in film cameras were constrained by a ten-minute time limit in the 1940s. Therefore, every ten minutes (or so) in the film, Hitchcock had to invent an ingenious solution for where to place his camera, so he could replace the film stock without any visible edit. He would pan onto an actor's back to help disguise the reel change, or employ some similar solution.[6] But Hitchcock wasn't the only auteur to fully embrace constraint as a means to explore new potentials. Welles believed strongly in the power of constraints and has been quoted as saying, "The enemy of art is the absence of limitations" (McBride 2006, 254). It is probably no coincidence that Welles's *Touch of Evil,* the most highly self-conscious film noir, was a deliberate attempt by the famed director to prove he could work effectively in the confines of the Hollywood studio system, making the film a de facto demonstration that such constraints stimulated him as an artist.

Self-consciousness and constraint also go hand in hand in current films noir, which often structure their narratives around overt citations of earlier noir visual, and hard-boiled literary, source material. The narrative sequences of *Kiss Kiss Bang Bang* (2005) derive their titles, and to some degree their diegetic action, from works by Raymond Chandler, and the film opens with a voice-over narrating a playful flashback to how the film's protagonist became, quite by accident, a crime film star. Likewise, three of the Coen brothers' finest films, their so-called "noir trilogy" of *Miller's Crossing* (1989), *The Big Lebowski* (1998), and *The Man Who Wasn't There* (2001), are their tributes to the hard-boiled masters Hammett, Chandler, and James M. Cain, respectively, and the films bear many self-conscious traces of reuse and re-working of the source material.[7] *The Man Who Wasn't There* operates under the additional constraint of being shot in black and white, and the choice of shooting a black-and-white noir picture in 2001 might be considered a self-conscious reversal of the constraints governing classic B films noir, which were forced to use black-and-white stock because of the limited availability and high cost of color stock in wartime Hollywood.

One of the best discussions of this constraint can be found in "Pansies Don't Float: Gay Representability, Film Noir, and *The Man Who Wasn't There*" by Vincent Brook and Allen Campbell:

> Of course, much has changed in the six decades between the releases of *Casablanca* and *The Man Who Wasn't There*. In the New Hollywood tradition of the artful genre pastiche (Neale; Bordwell 1985), *self-conscious intertextual allusion* is the name of the game. Now filmmaking *constraints* are more imposed by the filmmakers themselves than dictated by industrial norms. In *Man*, for example, shadowy sets and black-and-white photography, once necessitated by low budgets, are now daringly employed by "independent" auteurs in defiance of contemporary commercial aesthetics and even fiscal conservatism, as color film stock has become more readily and cheaply available. (Brook and Campbell 2003; emphasis ours)

Again, one has the sense of noir scholars discussing the particularly oulipian characteristics of noir but without the prerequisite knowledge of the Oulipo on which to hang the comment.

While there are, then, good historical reasons for viewing films noir as constrained texts in the oulipian sense, additional evidence of their oulipian nature can be found in the critical reception surrounding these films.

In their seminal book *The Classical Hollywood Cinema: Film Style and Mode of Production to 1960*, David Bordwell, Janet Staiger, and Kristin Thompson (hereafter BST) also speak of classical Hollywood cinema as a body of constrained texts. This was, they suggest, an "excessively obvious cinema" wherein "the system cannot determine every minute detail of the work . . .

(but) it isolates preferred practices and sets limits upon invention" (1985, 4). Within such a system, "quality" was derived not from engaging in avant-garde practices or in "violating a norm" but rather from "modifying or skill-fully obeying the premise of a dominant style" (6). Ultimately, BST's analysis of one hundred randomly selected Hollywood films suggests that a range of constraints—technical, stylistic, generic, and cultural—played a powerful role in the development of film style in Hollywood.[8] As BST put it at the beginning of their study, "Before there are auteurs, there are constraints" (4).

But within this discussion of formally constrained classical film texts, BST specifically explore the "case" of film noir, "often regarded as the most deeply problematic group of films produced in Hollywood" (1985, 75). Reading noir through their exhaustive articulation of a constrained mode of production in classical Hollywood cinema, BST seek to proleptically respond to what others might see as film noir's apparent nonconformity to their critical paradigm. They claim that noir films have attracted "critical attention because they attack certain American values prominent in mainstream Hollywood cinema" (75); they go on to depict noir largely as a category created by film critics searching for "traits" that would constitute "a unified grouping, or série" (75).[9] While they admit that "issues of transgression and subversion, stylization and realism, foreign influence and domestic genre intersect in that body of work known as film noir" (74), BST's ultimate aim is to explain how this category of film can be read within the limits of their methodology:

> Formally and stylistically, all . . . of film noir's challenges none the less adhere to specific and non-subversive conventions. . . . The case of film noir can be solved by investigating realistic and generic motivation. . . . The crucial point . . . is that formally and technically these noir films remained codified: a minority practice, but a unified one. (1985, 76–77)

Such definitive statements give the impression BST were forced to address the noir style, sensing that films noir and noir scholarship posed particular challenges to the unity (and by extension, universality) of their critical model.

We would like to concur with BST that noir texts remain formally "codified," but this does not mean that they are "non-subversive" or that "the case of film noir can be solved by investigating realistic and generic motivation." The slippage at this moment in BST's thesis from a discussion of "constraint" as a means of production to a claim of a "codified" product would seem to suggest they are apprehensive about their solution to "the case of film noir" and feel the need to freeze their target as they aim their apparatus. For codification implies something static and controllable (a message further enforced by BST's choice of the verb "remain"), whereas "constrained" texts in the noir, or oulipian, sense remain infinitely variable and generative (precisely because they are constrained) and evince self-consciousness and playfulness that are deeply subversive in ways that can't be easily codified.

BST's maneuver here is similar to many we've seen in scholarship surrounding oulipian texts. Critics set up a rigorous structure for discussing the formalism of these works, and then begin to intuit the texts' transgressive potential and scramble to bracket it off in various ways: the text is *nothing but* evidence of the formal constraint that produced it; the text's form is an embodiment of some historical/cultural transgression so profound and traumatic that the author cannot tackle it with his conscious mind (a reading of form that undercuts any genius on the author's part and gives it over to the critic who can see what the author could not).[10] Even those readers who do recognize the self-consciousness of oulipian texts rarely acknowledge how such self-consciousness is deliberate and patterned in ways similar to any critical reading.

In other words, BST are right to point out that, in the case of film noir, new and inventive results came from so thoroughly embracing the constraints of the system, not from trying to subvert them. In this sense, film noir is the ultimate proof of the genius of a constrained studio system, an example of filmmaking that is born of "modifying or skillfully obeying the premise of a dominant style." But films noir (like oulipian texts) actually become more subversive as they become more constrained.

This is because they obey constraint in a very self-conscious fashion, and the formal traces of this self-consciousness *play* all over the surface of these films. Thus, critics are forced to articulate qualifications and caveats (often while claiming to defend what is so distinctive about films noir) because what these constrained texts "transgress" and "subvert" with their formalism is not classical filmmaking but rather any criticism of classical filmmaking that fails to recognize what these films do to critically read themselves. Noir subverts and transgresses the work of the critic who believes his intervention is somehow crucial to the understanding of classical filmmaking—just as Warren Motte's translation of "Mathews's Algorithm" was subverted, in the very first line of translation, by that algorithm's ability (and Mathews's ability, in describing that algorithm) to generate both narrative and analysis. Thus, we would suggest BST would have done more to advance our understanding of noir (and even of classical Hollywood cinema as a whole) if they had not attempted to "solve" the case of noir but had instead offered up their investigative notes and then let the films give their own confessions. For their solution ends up delimiting the creative and critical potentials of constraint.

Not surprisingly, then, noir studies are bogged down by the same critical lacunae as studies of classical Hollywood filmmaking and studies of the Oulipo. As we have seen, a few scholars have acknowledged noir's self-consciousness—with caveats. Todd Erickson, for example, asserts, "Film noir, at its inception was an innocent, unconscious cinematic reaction to the popular culture of its time. The contemporary film noir is self-conscious, and well aware of its heritage" ([1995] 1996, 323). This would seem to be in keeping with Thomas Schatz's contention that, in the evolutionary process of cinema's need for generic variation, both filmmakers and audiences grow increasingly sensitive to the formal makeup of genre films. But Schatz acknowledges that both filmmakers and audiences in the forties and fifties were highly attuned to film noir's "rules of expression and composition," which led to "self-reflexive or formally self-conscious films, genre films which parody or subvert the genre's essential pro-social stance, the tendency for foreign filmmakers to utilize a genre's formal features as aesthetic ends in themselves with little regard for their social function, and so on" (1981, 264). In other words, films noir started out as highly self-conscious and only became more so.[11]

Rarely have critics considered how the self-consciousness of noir texts creates something akin to criticism. And to our knowledge, no one has argued, in the manner we do here, that the carefully structured self-consciousness of films noir (and oulipian texts) constitutes auto-exegesis. Among the few studies that have critically assessed noir's self-consciousness are Foster Hirsch's *The Dark Side of the Screen: Film Noir* (with its wonderful take on *Touch of Evil* as "noir's rococo tombstone") and *Detours and Lost Highways: A Map of Neo-noir*, and Tom Conley's view of noir as a textual space in a chapter of *Film Hieroglyphs* entitled "Decoding Film Noir." Not surprisingly, these works share an important focus; both frame discussions of the self-consciousness of noir in terms of discussions of space. They see these films creating something of a text map, a parallel narrative within the narrative that is often at odds with the diegetic action in revealing ways.

These arguments recall Le Lionnais's comment that oulipian constraints draw on mathematical procedures that allow for topological exploration of textual space[12] and our own contention that such textual exploration leaves in its wake both a narrative and a critical commentary about that narrative.[13] For example, in the case of Perec's *A Void*, highly formalized and self-conscious puns and intertextual allusions structure an extradiegetic space from which the text charts the creative interplay of form and diegetic action.

At this point, it seems fair to conclude that, in their modes of production, critical reception, and penchant for self-reflection, films noir are in many ways similar to oulipian texts.[14] In order to read them as we have *A Void*—which is to say, in order to understand how they enact readings of themselves—the challenge is to discover what self-conscious gestures they make that function analogously to Perec's intertextual allusions and self-conscious puns.

After watching these films noir a great many times, we've decided the best answer to that question might be . . . intertextual allusions and self-conscious puns.[15] These films do not borrow from one another *simply* because budget constraints forced them to do so. They stage their borrowings with a wink to the viewer. They borrow not just stock footage but also storylines, character traits, and methods of lighting and composing shots—and in each case they screen their theft in ways that reflect their knowledge that such appropriation is an act that creates both narrative and a commentary upon that narrative.[16]

Like Edgar Allan Poe's "The Purloined Letter," they leave the evidence in plain sight.

Rather than trying to understand the product through the history of its composition, or read the very letter of the auteur's intention (an impossibility, for as Poe has shown, it shall remain sealed to our view), let us explore what the act itself, and the careful disposition of evidence, reveals about how these narratives structure and read themselves.[17] For through a geometrically (i.e., topologically) precise composition of shots and self-conscious acts of intertextual borrowing, these films formulate a "geometry of auto-exegesis" that allows them to explore and map their own topology—the total space of their narrative.[18]

If the critic does not see, or acknowledge, the ways these texts read themselves, he is forced to bracket them off—a gesture that may seem to protect his carefully constructed paradigm but in point of fact constructs the gallows from which he hangs himself.[19] If he accepts that these films enact auto-exegesis, he is forced to find the evidence. No easy task, as it's so plainly in sight as to be almost invisible.

Chapter 5 is the evidence. We're constructing our case by identifying those moments when films noir seem to be giving some sort of confession of their artistic pilferings and structural crimes by laying out the goods. We're helping these moments to speak by taking them out of their normal context —not by placing them in an interrogation room where we coerce them into stating the "facts" we already suspect to be true but rather by using oulipian impulses (if not actual oulipian constraints) to free them to express both their diegetic and their extradiegetic motives, their playful and their deadly serious thoughts.

5

Oufinopo

The Noiremes

There's never any telling what you'll say or do next, except that it's bound to be something astonishing.— *The Maltese Falcon* (1941)

If you are mean enough to *steal* from the *blind,* help yourself.— *Touch of Evil* (1958)

That rug really tied the room together.— *The Big Lebowski* (1998)

I N CHAPTER 4, we established that films noir, like oulipian texts, utilize particular forms of self-conscious constraint to simultaneously construct diegetic action and extradiegetic commentary upon that action. The task that remained was to identify filmic moments that seemed to do this openly, and to give them a context in which the full potential of their self-consciousness could be critically and creatively explored.[1]

Sometimes these moments were visual (in the composition or lighting of a frame, the use of a visual motif, or the expression of an actor), sometimes sonic (in a line of dialogue, a moment in the score, a diegetic noise, or a voice-over). Because we were limited by the print medium, we were forced in each case to find an image that stood in for this moment, even if the moment was sonic. But far from being a limitation, this proved to be an inspiring constraint as we articulated our understanding of what a given moment in the film had to say for itself.

Each bit of evidence we are about to enter into the record is thus composed of an image (or two), accompanied by our investigative notes on what confession we think is being made by the film moment the image is standing in for. We dubbed these bits of evidence "noiremes," for the suffix "-eme" defines the category comprising various elements of the item to which the suffix is added. And we found the term "noireme" to be as irresistible as the films themselves.

These bits of evidence are like the "known quantities" Harry Mathews runs through his algorithm—"groups of heterogeneous elements" drawn from (and, in the case of our investigative notes, inspired by) a given sample set of texts. This lead us to suspect that, if we were to dispose of them according to oulipian procedures, we would be engaging in an act of "lecture potentielle (qui) a le charme de faire ressortir la duplicité des textes" (potential reading [that] has the charm of making manifest the duplicity of texts") (1988, 91). For as Mathews argued, the resultants of such a systematic constraint for recombining texts can simultaneously create new narratives and enact analysis, thereby revealing both the creative and critical potentials of noir.[2]

As we assembled this manuscript, two questions remained. How would we delimit our sample set? How would we organize it? Obviously, we needed to find solutions like oulipian constraints to both questions.

A simple mathematical constraint helped us make the determination. We decided to add the total running time of the set of films that interested us (as discussed in chapter 1) and divide by the number of films in the set. The average running time of the films in the sample set was approximately 102.087 minutes, so we limited ourselves to 102 noiremes.[3]

Our sample set of 102 noiremes also consciously recalls that these films fit within the time constraints of commercial exhibition practices in U.S. cinemas in the 1940s and 1950s, a constraint that operated on filmmakers, just like the number of lines in a sonnet act upon a poet. Noir filmmakers knew their films needed to be of a certain length (more or less) and that temporal constraint was one of many constraints that allowed them to explore the *potential* of noir—a potential we investigate through the following experiment.

Once we'd selected our sample set of "heterogeneous elements," the question was how to organize them. We considered running them through Mathews's algorithm, but the large number of noiremes-as-variables made that impractical. We settled on the elementary constraint of running time percentage (RTP). Thus, a noireme born of filmic material that occurred at the five-minute mark of a two-hour film (RTP = 300 seconds ÷ 7,200 seconds, or 0.042) would precede a noireme inspired by material at the five-minute mark of a ninety-minute film (RTP = 0.056). The constraint forced us to rearrange these 102 noiremes (taken from thirty-one different films) and place them in the order in which they would have appeared on screen if together they formed some "master narrative," some complete confession.

We leave it to the reader to judge what the facts reveal about noir and judge the *potential* of this constraint (in the oulipian and nonoulipian senses) for the further analysis of existing noir texts and the creation of new noir films. Due to the nature of a printed book, we can only show one resultant of our constraint. Of course, all oulipian texts are but one resultant of a carefully calculated constraint. We would encourage readers to enter new evidence into this current constraint or to create new constraints. Both types of investigation promise to yield new information.

READING THE EVIDENCE

Each noireme comprises an even-numbered page and an odd-numbered page. On the even-numbered page, you will find one or two images that stand in for an *iconic moment* in the photography, sound, or dialogue of a given film noir. When the moment under consideration is photographic, the exact image in question is reproduced. When the iconic moment is in the sound or dialogue, we chose an image that occurs concurrently with that moment, or an image that occurs in close proximity to that moment and seems to capture it.

On the odd-numbered page, you will find our "investigative notes," that is, our thoughts on what that film moment has to say for itself. Under each of these notes is a reference to the podcast episode in which we also explore these thoughts, often at greater length.

In addition to these primary components, you will find the following information associated with the noiremes.

On the even-numbered page:

- A number for each noireme from 1 to 102
- The title of the film from which the image is taken
- The year of the film's release

- N = the time signature of the still images taken from each film, written as hh:mm:ss (hh = hours, mm = minutes, and ss = seconds)[4]
- RT = the running time of the film, written as hh:mm:ss[5]
- RTP = running time percentage, which is determined by taking N as percentage of RT (written as a percentage, expressed out to a thousandth of a percent)

On the odd-numbered page:

- A descriptive title for the copy that follows
- Our "investigative notes" about the moment under consideration
- The name of the person who articulated the thought, designated by our initials: SC for Shannon Clute and RE for Richard Edwards
- The episode number of the podcast that also investigates the film in question
- The date the podcast was published to the Internet

Noireme 001: *Sunset Blvd.* (1950)

N = 00:00:05 ‖ RT = 01:50:12 ‖ RTP = 00.076%

What is the opening shot of *Sunset Blvd.?* If it has been a while since you have seen the film, you will probably answer that it's an image of William Holden's character floating face down in a swimming pool. While that might be one of the most powerful images in the film, it is not the first image. The film actually begins with a slow camera dolly—in close-up—gliding across the gray anonymity of a concrete surface until it reaches the end of a street and we see the words "Sunset Blvd." These words appear diegetically within the story world, spray painted in chunky stenciling on the curb of Sunset Boulevard, and when we first read these words we are already "in the gutter." We are already where the sidewalk ends. When the camera begins to move again as part of the opening credits, the film does not choose to show us the magnificent mansions, the manicured lawns, and the towering palm trees of the ten thousand block of Sunset Blvd. Rather, it keeps our face close to the pavement. We are going to be seeing this world for what it really is; the camera is telling us not to get our hopes up too high. This is a world where dreams have enfolded into themselves. This is a world of decay. This is a world where "you can tell a man's fortunes by looking at his heels and knowing the score." The gray pavement seems to offer the hope we might be traveling, going someplace special, that—as we sit immobile in front of the screen—the Hollywood spectacular and its glamorous protagonists are going to bring us someplace. But ultimately, *Sunset Blvd.* never lets us out of the gutter.

RE
Episode 21 || 04/15/06

Noireme 002: *The Asphalt Jungle* (1950)

N = 00:00:14 ‖ RT = 01:52:04 ‖ RTP = 00.208%

The Asphalt Jungle opens with an extreme long shot of a diagonal, concrete stretch of urban space, introducing us to a dull, gray world that is out of kilter —an imbalanced world. Each character in the film will be introduced at some level of disequilibrium, whether it is newly released convict/muscle Dix Handley (Sterling Hayden), his girlfriend Doll Conovan (Jean Hagen), mastermind Doc Riedenschneider (Sam Jaffe), lawyer Alonzo Emmerich (Louis Calhern), or others in this fine ensemble cast. The large cast allows director John Huston to have multiple centers of disequilibrium that connect with each other as the ensemble prepares a complex jewelry store heist. God may not play dice with the universe, but John Huston surely does.

RE
Episode 8 || 10/01/05

Noireme 003: *The Killers* (1946)

N = 00:00:14 ‖ RT = 01:52:04 ‖ RTP = 00.280%

The opening moments of *The Killers* remind us of noir's tremendous economy in moving from a general atmosphere or situation to a fundamental question of human existence. The opening shot is from the backseat of a car, at night, and the men in the front seat are simply two shadows: they're hats, black against the headlights and the pavement before them. They're driving too fast, and we have a sense of coming in from behind the action, of being caught up in something beyond our control, something too poorly illuminated and moving too fast for us to understand. In other words, we, the viewers, are a lot like Burt Lancaster's character "The Swede."

SC
Episode 10 || 11/01/05

Noireme 004: *D.O.A.* (1950)

N = 00:00:20 ‖ RT = 01:23:32 ‖ RTP = 00.399%

N = 00:00:50

THE MAN IN CHARGE

D.O.A. opens with a shot of City Hall in Los Angeles at night. A man enters the frame from the side, and we see just his back in a dark suit. He walks with determination to City Hall. The camera follows him as he walks through the corridors, he asks a police officer on duty some question, and the officer gestures with his thumb. It then follows him down a long, dark hallway, as the opening credits are rolling, to the Homicide Bureau. He enters and says he wants to see the man in charge; they indicate where that man can be found. He steps in and says he wants to report a murder. The man in charge asks who was murdered, and he says, "I was." That is the first moment—when Frank Bigelow (Edmond O'Brien) announces that he is the dead man—that we see his face. This sequence demonstrates director Rudolph Maté's ability to use the camera to involve the audience in the story but also underscores that what might appear to be a very quirky noir is in fact typical in one fundamental sense: we believe we're being shown a capable and determined protagonist as he strides down the hall—a world-wise man who can deal with anything—but what we actually have on our hands is a dead man.

SC
Episode 27 || 09/01/06

Noireme 005: *Kiss Me Deadly* (1955)

N = 00:00:27 ‖ RT = 01:46:02 ‖ RTP = 00.424%

The 1955 film *Kiss Me Deadly* opens from the waist down. All we see initially is a pair of bare feet, running down the centerline of a two-lane highway. On the soundtrack, we hear the breathy gasps of a woman. The scene then cuts to a medium shot, and we see Christina Bailey's (Cloris Leachman) frantic expressions as she continues running. Then director Robert Aldrich pulls the camera farther away from Christina and again captures her running toward it. The effect is striking because it forces us to pay attention to what comes into the field of view: a desperate woman in a trench coat and bare feet, framed within the desolate nonspace of the highway, accentuated by a pitch-black sky reminiscent of a Weegee photograph. The score by Frank De Vol is equally powerful, played in a syncopated beat that accentuates the anxiety in these opening moments. Christina is clearly running from something as she tries to wave down any oncoming car on a deserted highway. Down this two-lane blacktop comes private eye Mike Hammer (Ralph Meeker), and in her desperation, Christina Bailey decides on a high-stakes gamble: she stands dead center of the highway and braces herself for either a ride or a deadly impact. At the last second, Mike Hammer sees her, swerves his car, and runs into a ditch. Both survive, and as they make their initial eye contact, Christina's continued gasps blur the erotic and the neurotic — sex and death.

RE
Episode 32 || 02/01/07

Noireme 006: *The Hitch-Hiker* (1953)

N = 00:00:39 || RT = 01:10:43 || RTP = 00.919%

The Hitch-Hiker drops us right into the action. Before the opening credits, we have a still of the pavement with the legs of a hitchhiker standing on the shoulder, and superimposed on this image are the following words: "This is a true story of a man and a gun and a car. The gun belonged to the man. The car might have been yours—or that young couple across the aisle. What you will see in the next seventy minutes could have happened to you. For the facts are actual." The RKO emblem comes in with the score and we cut to the title, superimposed on the image of a revolver pointed at the audience. We cut back to the leather jacket and boots beside the highway, but this time the figure is walking as the opening credits begin to roll. In his slow gait, there is something ominous, inevitable. Someone picks him up, they drive off, the scene cuts to nighttime. The car comes to a stop, the boots we saw before climb out, a woman screams, a gun fires twice, and a purse hits the ground. The boots walk away and it grows dark, then a flashlight comes back the other way. The sheriff finds the murder scene. A newspaper headline spins in focus and the manhunt is on. This was still a fresh narrative style at the time: gone is the omnipresent protagonist who drove the action. Instead, we have the faceless, shadowy figure of crime that invades every space, even the space of the cinema, imposing a terrible reality of the present. It is a quasi-documentary style that forces the spectator to consider the horrors of violence rather than sit back and see it as good entertainment. This film came out in a political climate not unlike our own, when liberalism was framed as dangerous antipatriotism, violence was too often given a glossy sheen, and we wanted to believe our political heroes were above corruption. While these themes exceed the film's action, we can only fully understand the film's crisis of identity and sense of dread in this larger sociopolitical context—and with the knowledge that it was created by a marginalized, and in some cases blacklisted, group of artists. Part of the genius of Ida Lupino's film was that it tapped the mood so profoundly as to make the spectator question the world she lived in, without throwing in the political framework that might bias viewing.

SC

Episode 7 || 09/15/05

Noireme 007: *Touch of Evil* (1958)

N = 00:01:08 ‖ RT = 01:50:41 ‖ RTP = 01.024%

N = 00:05:00

The opening shot of *Touch of Evil* couldn't be more to the point. It's an incredible three-minute-and-twenty-second tracking shot on a crane, where the picture opens with a close-up of a bomb in someone's hands. The person sets the timer on the bomb and puts it in the trunk of a car, then a couple comes from around the corner of a building and climbs into the car. The shot then raises up in the air, giving us the sensation of this being an omniscient camera; and, indeed, that's exactly what it is in the hands of Orson Welles. The camera then goes over the top of a dark building and drops down the front of it, past the edge of the roof and the neon signs, and precedes the car as it works its way slowly through a traffic- and pedestrian-clogged city in Mexico. This shot is visually inventive and builds incredible narrative tension, for we know the car is in the middle of downtown, and we know it has a bomb ticking in its trunk. This is the scene that director Welles pleaded to have reinstated, because in its original release version, the studio ran the film's credits over this scene.* It does not seem too much of a stretch to argue that this is explicitly a scene intended to blow up the conventions of noir filmmaking, and that this film is often considered the last film noir of the classical noir period because it is so self-conscious, so full of visual puns, that it ultimately explodes any possibility from this point forward of making a un-self-conscious noir film.

SC
Episode 31 || 01/01/07

---

* The 1958 theatrical release of *Touch of Evil* had the film's opening credits run over this scene against the wishes of Welles. However, most viewers today are more familiar with this opening sequence without credits, due to a 1998 restoration project, led by film editor Walter Murch. In the restored version, based on a famous fifty-eight-page memo written by Welles himself, the credits have been removed (along with the Henry Mancini score in the opening sequence), restoring, as much as possible, Welles's original vision for this magical visual moment.

Noireme 008: *Out of the Past* (1947)

N = 00:01:10 || RT = 01:36:38 || RTP = 01.207%

N = 00:01:35

Typically in film noir, as in the hard-boiled fiction that so influenced it, the city is omnipresent—a dark place of greed, corruption, and violence. Instead, *Out of the Past* begins with a series of long shots of landscapes absolutely saturated with light. There is a pastoral, idyllic present (that will contrast with, and increasingly be invaded by, a dark, urban past). It is in this natural landscape that we first see protagonist Jeff Bailey (Robert Mitchum) and his belle Anne Miller (Virginia Huston). We are tricked into thinking this might be a typical love story, but the past is always lurking and soon comes looking, in the person of actor Paul Valentine. Jeff Bailey is pulled back into a sordid affair he never really could leave behind, and as the film progresses, both the tale and the scene grow darker.

SC
Episode 1 || 07/02/05

Noireme 009: *The Set-Up* (1949)

N = 00:01:20 ‖ RT = 01:12:27 ‖ RTP = 01.840%

N = 01:11:59

The story of *The Set-Up* follows washed-up boxer Stoker Thompson (Robert Ryan), who is literally fighting for his life in his last boxing match. The duration of the diegesis is the same as the actual running length of the film: it takes seventy-two minutes to watch the film, and there are seventy-two minutes of continuous real-time action in the on-screen story. The temporal design of *The Set-Up* recalls other films noir in the classical era that experimented with the formal properties of noir storytelling, such as *The Lady in the Lake*. And while *The Lady in the Lake* is well known for its use of a first-person point of view, in *The Set-Up* it is Robert Wise's editing style and concise story construction that convey a powerful sense of realism. Through the conceit of real-time storytelling, the audience is constantly reminded that time is running out for Stoker Thompson.

RE
Episode 18 || 03/01/06

Noireme 010: *Chinatown* (1974)

N = 00:02:28 || RT = 02:10:25 || RTP = 01.891%

N = 00:00:24

As a *noir en couleur, Chinatown* presented a very interesting set of challenges to the film's director Roman Polanski and cinematographer John Alonzo. Instead of filming *Chinatown* as a nostalgic black-and-white film, Polanski and Alonso chose to film the story in color and, in doing so, created the color palette that has been influential on the look of neo-noir filmmaking ever since. First, *Chinatown*'s color palette is dominated by natural colors: browns and shades of orange from the earth; a muted blue color from the sky; a foamy surf color from the sea. Second, *Chinatown* desaturates these colors, an aesthetic choice that runs counter to the typical film set in sunny Southern California. The color of the film is desaturated by mixing in blacks and grays to bring down all the color values (into darker hues and shades). Using this technique, Polanski is being true to film noir: these natural colors, at their heart, are being *slashed* with black and grey.

RE

Once you understand it in these terms, as being "slashed," you will see that Polanski reveals this trick at the very beginning of the film. The opening credits have a background of diagonal lines in shades of brown, bordering on grey, bordering on an orangey brown, bordering on black—very muted slashing lines. They are stationary, but as the white credits scroll from the bottom of the screen upward, it plays a trick on the eye. We start to think these diagonal lines are moving horizontally across the screen, but it's an illusion created by the movement of the letters against the diagonal background. Polanski is clueing us into the way he has slashed the color palette for the film, but he's also clueing us into the fact that the visual style of this film is going to be tied to the narrative content. How? *Chinatown* is a tale of deception, and despite all the apparent forward motion, things end up pretty much as they began, for corruption is immovable.

SC
Episode 24 || 05/31/06

Noireme 011: *Gun Crazy* (1950)

N = 00:01:45 ‖ RT = 01:27:01 ‖ RTP = 02.011%

N = 00:02:43

If you want to understand the powerful sense of impotence that defined America's young men post-World War II, watch Joseph Lewis's 1950 masterpiece *Gun Crazy*. The opening shot is of a rain-soaked town at night, a street corner, but close-up so that you can't quite see where you're coming from or where you're going. A neon hotel sign beckons in the background, then a boy comes around the corner. Soaked, and with an obsessed look in his eyes, he comes up to the window of a gun shop. The camera pulls back, and that's when you realize that the opening shot was through the window of the gun shop, thereby placing the audience with the guns, and making us wonder if this boy's obsession with gunplay coincides with a desperate need to be seen, to have an audience. The boy breaks the window, grabs a gun and ammunition, and runs off. He trips. The gun skids across the wet pavement and lands at the sheriff's feet. There's an extreme close-up, low-angle shot up at the serious face of Justice, then a medium-long shot of the boy face down on the wet pavement in the rain that zooms into a close-up, where we see the fear and shame on his face that will define his life. Cut to the courtroom. His older sister defends him as the judge discusses his obsession for guns. He sits, shamefaced, staring at his feet. The huge shadow of the witness chair, projected on the wall in front of him, dwarfs him. A high-angle shot down at the face of his sister Ruby, who is indeed a gem, shows her in medium close-up—serious, frank, and bathed in light. That same angle leaves the boy small, relegated to a corner in the background, as if he's caught in a funhouse where everything is proportioned too large for him, and he simply can't live up to expectations. He is literally and figuratively smaller than the generation just a few years older than he.

SC
Episode 17 || 02/15/06

Noireme 012: *The Lady from Shanghai* (1947)

N = 00:01:50 ‖ RT = 01:27:26 ‖ RTP = 02.097%

N = 00:15:25

CUT AND DYED

In *The Lady from Shanghai,* Orson Welles executes a complete and total makeover of leading lady Rita Hayworth, which is an unexpected choice. At the time of *The Lady from Shanghai*'s release, Rita Hayworth is one of the most famous stars in Hollywood: she is "Gilda," the ultimate femme fatale in film noir. In that earlier film, she has her trademark long, red hair, and director Charles Vidor uses it to emphasize her glamour and beauty. Yet when Orson Welles casts Hayworth in *The Lady from Shanghai,* he cuts her hair and dyes it a color he dubbed "topaz blond." On one level, this operated as a publicity stunt for the picture. But in terms of the film itself, Welles is deglamorizing and manipulating his actors: he literally "de-gilda-izes" Hayworth and makes her something other than her successful, established screen persona. The purposefulness of this decision can be seen in relation to Welles's framing of other characters in the film. For example, Grisby (Glenn Anders) is frequently shot in extreme "choker" close-up with a puffy, perspiring face, making his character more repulsive. At the same time, Welles keeps the camera at a distance from Elsa Bannister (Hayworth), who is almost always framed in medium-long shot. This creates a strange set of alternations and tensions, where the audience gets closest to the most grotesque characters and is kept away from the most glamorous.

RE
Episode 15 || 01/15/06

Noireme 013: *Murder, My Sweet* (1944)

N = 00:02:19 || RT = 01:46:02 || RTP = 02.185%

Murder, My Sweet begins with a blindfolded Philip Marlowe (Dick Powell), narrating a story in flashback. In other words, our narrator literally can no longer see. Not only does *Murder, My Sweet* begin by highlighting the narrator's *restricted* vision, but it also keeps the audience in the dark as to the source of his blindness until the end of the film. Additionally, Marlowe loses consciousness three times during the course of the film, implying multiple moments of lost time and lost memory. All of these devices foreground that Marlowe does not have his faculties fully in order and indicate he may not be a reliable narrator.

RE

Chandler's stories take a while to get rolling, and that's largely due to the first-person point of view in the narration. We don't have flashbacks; we get the story in real time as the private investigator (PI) works through it. Some of the trails he goes down are dead ends, and obviously that can't happen with film. So what does Edward Dmytryk do? Flashback, but with a twist. A straightforward flashback implies too much knowledge at the outset from the first-person narrator, which would kill the suspense for the audience. So Dmytryk decides the narrator should be blindfolded and have had his eyes scorched by the powder of a gun that went off at close range. We're required to reconstruct the vision with someone whose vision has been damaged, and we get the narrative suspense of bumbling through the story although it's told in flashback.

SC
Episode 26 || 06/30/06

Noireme 014: *The Asphalt Jungle* (1950)

N = 00:2:28 || RT = 01:52:04 || RTP = 02.201%

In the evolution of John Huston's directing from *The Maltese Falcon* to *The Asphalt Jungle,* we see a movement toward the grit and imposing weight of urban reality. In 1950, the Best Cinematography Oscar went to Robert Krasker for *The Third Man.* That's interesting in this context, because one of the earliest shots in *The Asphalt Jungle* has Dix running away from the scene of a crime, through an urban landscape in ruins. It doesn't appear to be an American landscape but rather looks just like Vienna in *The Third Man.* It's an entirely different city from the San Francisco we're shown in *The Maltese Falcon.* In that film, granted, San Francisco was a city where crime could occur, but it was still glamorous and beautiful. The unnamed city of *The Asphalt Jungle* is neither. It's a shell of a city.

SC
Episode 8 || 10/01/05

Noireme 015: *Notorious* (1946)

N = 00:03:04 ‖ RT = 01:42:08 ‖ RTP = 03.003%

N = 00:11:51

By casting Cary Grant and Ingrid Bergman in the lead roles in *Notorious,* Alfred Hitchcock does something that goes against the film noir aesthetic; he uses actors for whom there is no substitute. These are two of the most glamorous stars in Hollywood in 1946—the suave and debonair Grant and the sublimely beautiful Bergman. Together, this is a star couple of greatness. And yet Hitchcock, the wily craftsman, introduces them against type. Initially, we don't see Bergman at her glamorous best, and we don't see Grant at his cocktail party most splendid. Instead, we get an initial glimpse of Alicia (Bergman) as she walks out of a courtroom in which her father has just been convicted of treason against the United States, against the crush and the press of the paparazzi. And we get another early shot of Alicia waking up hung over, her fake hairpiece in bed next to her, completely disheveled, with dark circles around her eyes. The first shot of Devlin (Grant) is the back of his head—a staggering shot. It's hard to imagine casting Grant in a film and introducing his character by showing the audience the back of his head.

SC

Moreover, Devlin doesn't immediately speak. One thing instantly recognizable about Grant is the way he talks. Devlin is introduced as both a silent and shadowy figure. *Notorious* starts by putting the audience in this very uncomfortable position. These are actors to whom we are powerfully cathected, to whom we transfer our desires. Hitchcock knows that. So what does he do with our identification with stars? He uses it to twist a knife in our back. Grant's Devlin is enigmatic but also sadistic in the way that he physically, verbally, and emotionally abuses Alicia. Likewise, Bergman plays a deeply unsympathetic character in Alicia: she's an alcoholic, a tramp, and the daughter of a traitor. Hitchcock gives us not star turns but noir turns.

RE
Episode 14 || 01/01/06

Noireme 016: *Blade Runner* (1982)

N = 00:04:00 ‖ RT = 01:56:27 ‖ RTP = 03.435%

N = 00:04:37

From the outset, it's clear that Ridley Scott works to establish *Blade Runner* as a noir. The film opens with a series of quick cuts that are initially disorienting. The first thing the viewer sees after the opening credits (which are all in black and white) is a futuristic landscape, with what look to be refinery flares popping against the night sky. It's a science fiction cityscape, not anywhere we recognize as here and now. We cut to an interior scene, dimly lit. We see a man in a suit silhouetted against the faint light coming in through a window, fan blades turning up above and cigarette smoke rising through the frame—a quintessential noir shot. We cut back to the cityscape, this time further forward, and we're starting to see a pyramidal building that dominates the cityscape. We cut back to the interior scene, only this time the camera is pulled back a little, and we see the man standing near a computer that rests on the table. What was initially pure noir in its vision is now noir with a futuristic spin. Again, we cut to the exterior shot, this time close to the pyramid, and then again to the interior, where we now see almost the entire room. It's a modern room, very futuristic. We realize in retrospect that through this series of quick cuts a landscape that would otherwise seem foreign and unapproachable is made approachable. Scott "pulls back" into the conventions of noir to make the unfamiliar future he is advancing us into seem more familiar: the radical stylization of noir has become a grounding force of realism.

SC
Episode 6 || 09/01/05

Noireme 017: *Murder, My Sweet* (1944)

N = 00:03:51 ‖ RT = 01:46:02 ‖ RTP = 03.631%

N = 00:03:53

Edward Dmytryk's direction of *Murder, My Sweet* is masterful, blending the grittiness typical of B films noir with the elaborately choreographed and executed shots more characteristic of A pictures. With the initial voice-over, we see scenes of a dirty and imposing LA like that in *He Walked by Night*. But if we pay attention, we realize Dmytryk shoots the city from uncommon angles that make it look like an active player in the story—a force that looms over us. The scene cuts to Philip Marlowe's (Dick Powell) office as his glib and ironic voice-over continues. He's looking out the window, and there's a neon sign flashing outside. Whenever that flash comes on, everything in the background of his office disappears. When the flash fades, the ambient light of his office brings out the office interior in reflection in the windowpane. It's in such a reflection that Dmytryk introduces us to the character Moose Malloy (Mike Mazurki). As the neon fades, we see his reflection framed in the window; then the neon comes on again, and Malloy disappears. This careful framing not only sets up the intrigue but also gives us the sense that Malloy is a pale reflection of what he used to be, before he suffered the loss that has driven him to a private eye. By extension, it reminds us that all of these men are in a fragile position—framed as they are on the brittle glass, against the incessant and incandescent dangers of the modern city.

SC
Episode 26 || 06/30/06

Noireme 018: *The Postman Always Rings Twice* (1946)

N = 00:04:34 || RT = 01:52:50 || RTP = 04.047%

The film *The Postman Always Rings Twice* departs in significant ways from the novel by the same title on which it is based. The characters are not nearly so flawed, nearly so average, as they are in Cain's original work. In the novel, Cora is introduced in this way: "Except for the shape, she really wasn't any raving beauty. But she had a sulky look to her, and her lips stuck out in a way that made me want to mash them for her." All we have to do to know what went wrong in the film adaptation is think about that description of Cora, and then see the introduction of Lana Turner's Cora in the film. We're getting Cain filtered through the dreamworks of MGM. We can't help but wonder if this would have been a better film if made by Warner Brothers, with whom John Garfield did most of his early pictures and from whom he got a release to do this film. Or better yet, had it been made by RKO, or one of the poverty-row studios, it would likely have been something much closer to Cain's novel. What MGM gives us might best be termed "glamour noir," as the introduction of Cora shows. In the book, we first see her in her smock at a sink full of dirty dishes. In the film she's introduced when Garfield's character Frank is sitting at the counter at the diner. We hear a click, followed by the sound of something rolling. Frank turns to see an object rolling toward him. He leans and picks it up, and the camera tilts through a dense network of shadows to the legs of Turner. Initially, that's all we see—these incredibly long legs in short shorts. Then we cut back to Frank's expression and watch the breath be taken out of him by what he's seeing. Then we cut back to Cora in a glamorous outfit of short, white shorts, a halter-top, and some sort of turban. We're about as far as we can get from a woman in a smock doing a load of dirty dishes.

SC
Episode 30 || 12/01/06

Noireme 019: *The Grifters* (1990)

N = 00:04:40 ‖ RT = 01:50:19 ‖ RTP = 04.230%

The three main characters of Stephen Frears's *The Grifters* form a triangle—a common conceit in film noir that is done exceptionally well in this story. Roy Dillon (John Cusack) is a short-con grifter, someone who is always working for the easy mark, without a partner, doing small-time grifting, swindling, and hustling (tricks like "the twenties," where he pays for the drinks and switches the bills out, or other small con jobs). He's currently dating Myra Langtry (Annette Bening), who we first see as a person pulling scams that involve the use of her body—a spider woman who uses her femininity and her sexuality to get her way. The trio is completed by Roy's mother, Lilly (Angelica Huston), a grifter who works with the East Coast rackets, running the playback scam at the racetrack. Frequently in films with this kind of triangulation, there's a desire to do something that is fairly theatrical—to stage the triangulation in the mise-en-scène. Here, director Stephen Frears comes up with a novel idea, which is to do a triple split screen. Instead of there being a single-shot geometric triangulation, there's a flattening of the triangle that accentuates the great similarities between these characters. When the three of them do a head turn, all in sunglasses, at the entrances to three different environments where they carry out their seemingly different activities, the split screen brings them all together in a moment of persuasive commonality. This shot gives us a means to read the whole film. Roy can never escape his explicit framing between these two women: it's a visual prison, a stamp of his destiny.

RE
Episode 16 || 02/01/06

Noireme 020: *Gun Crazy* (1950)

N = 00:04:12 ‖ RT = 01:27:01 ‖ RTP = 04.827%

N = 00:04:16

Gun Crazy opens with a series of scenes that establish Bart Tare (John Dall) as an emasculated character. He steals a gun to have a sense of power, immediately has it taken away by the sheriff, and then is shown shamefaced in court—small and powerless. Not only is there a line of dialogue at this moment that says, "Bart needs a man" in the family, but also everyone who comes to his defense in court is a woman. His sister vouches for him, telling the judge how Bart could never hurt anyone and relating the story of the trauma Bart suffered as a young child when he accidentally shot a little chick to death. When have we ever seen a person with a gun look as pathetic or as ruined as the young Bart Tare, who is completely emasculated the moment he kills the little chick? Moreover, when do films noir ever show us childhood? This one does, and a noir childhood ain't pretty.

RE
Episode 17 || 02/15/06

Noireme 021: *Double Indemnity* (1944)

N = 00:05:18 || RT = 01:47:32 || RTP = 04.929%

This story of *Double Indemnity* is told in flashback, and that flashback takes up the entire running time of the film except for a brief denouement. This simultaneously builds tension and lets the viewer know that even once she has all of the background she doesn't know how the story will end. It also shows that every man is a product of his past, and that is one of the most important themes of film noir. Early on, Walter Neff (Fred MacMurray) sits down at a Dictaphone and starts to tell his story. As is true of most hard-boiled detective fiction, he tells it in the first person, making the story immediate and approachable. Yet, he tells it through one level of mediation: he's speaking into the machine but intending to reach his friend and coworker Barton Keyes (Edward G. Robinson). This narrative device brings the spectator into the film; there is just this one machine that stands between Neff and Keyes, and likewise there is just the one machine—the camera—that stands between Neff and the audience (making us analogous in some ways to Keyes). This story is being told to us so we can unravel the mystery, just as it is being told to Keyes for the same reason.

SC

Neff's speaking into the Dictaphone also supplies the voice-over for the film, giving the viewer access to the character's subjective voice. There is nothing in Walter Neff's voice-over that indicates to the audience he has all the answers. This is not an omniscient narrator; this is a flawed narrator. Neff is telling the audience a tale of doom and woe, and one of the things that makes this genre so appealing is this idea there's nothing the character can do to stop the chain of events.

RE
Episode 2 || 07/08/05

Noireme 022: *Detour* (1945)

N = 00:03:50 ‖ RT = 01:07:46 ‖ RTP = 05.657%

N = 00:04:14

Edgar G. Ulmer's 1945 film *Detour* has long been praised as one of the finer, true B films noir—a film that overcame its low budget with artful minimalism and clever cinematography and thereby helped to establish the barren psychological world and stripped-down style that even bigger budget films would try to re-create. In his superlative book *More than Night: Film Noir in Its Contexts,* James Naremore highlights these qualities of *Detour* and, by way of example, discusses an early scene in the film when Al Roberts, played by Tom Neal, is down and out in a small diner. An all too familiar tune plays on the jukebox and sparks the memory of happier days. In Naremore's words, "The lights suddenly dim, signaling a transition into subjective mood. A spotlight hovers around Neal's eyes, giving him a demonic look, and for a moment we can sense a technician behind the camera, trying to aim the light correctly. Neal broods, and the camera tilts down to view his coffee cup; what it sees, however, is a model, several times larger than the original, looming up before him in vaguely surreal fashion. Few people will notice that a substitution of coffee cups has occurred; indeed they are not supposed to notice, because Ulmer wants to create a dreamlike close-up of an apparently ordinary object and thus set the stage for the nightmarish flashback" (2008, 147). While we agree with Naremore's reading, we would grant an even greater degree of technical mastery to this scene than he has. In our opinion, the wiggle of the light in Neal's eyes is not a mistake but rather an intentional gesture to call attention to the ways the camera and lighting help create the noir universe. This hardly seems too much to claim, for the giant coffee cup is likewise intentionally obtrusive and is, moreover, divided perfectly in half with light and shadow—like the noir universe itself. We would suggest that many moments in this film demonstrate a similarly high degree of self-consciousness and would argue that the film as a whole can be viewed less as *a* noir narrative than as *the* noir narrative, that *Detour* is less interested in telling a story than in demonstrating how noir stories are told. It might reasonably be called an allegory of noir, or a self-conscious noir metanarrative.

SC

Episode 29 || 11/01/06

Noireme 023: *The Big Sleep* (1946)

N = 00:07:03 ‖ RT = 01:53:51 ‖ RTP = 06.192%

An early scene in *The Big Sleep* demonstrates a new sensibility for introducing the "star" in postwar Hollywood films—especially films noir. *The Big Sleep* begins with Philip Marlowe (Humphrey Bogart) showing up at the mansion of the wealthy General Sternwood (Charles Waldron). As Marlowe enters the house, he is greeted by a valet who proceeds to bring him into a fancy and ornate interior parlor. In the next moment, we are introduced to one of the primary female characters, Carmen Sternwood (Martha Vickers). The initial meeting of Marlowe and Carmen is ripe with double entendres and witty banter, using dialogue from Raymond Chandler's source novel. After that encounter, Marlowe is brought to see General Sternwood. They meet in a hothouse behind the mansion. Instead of showing Bogart's Marlowe as the ultimate cool-under-fire, hard-boiled hero, or the suave leading man, director Howard Hawks uses a realistic setting to let the audience see Philip Marlowe sweat.

RE
Episode 11 || 11/15/05

Noireme 024: *The Maltese Falcon* (1941)

N = 00:06:58 || RT = 01:40:29 || RTP = 06.933%

There's an important scene in the movie *The Maltese Falcon* that doesn't occur in the book. Sam Spade's (Humphrey Bogart) partner, Archer (Jerome Cowan), has agreed to tail someone for a Miss Wonderly after she visits Spade and Archer's office. He does the tail job, and we see him in a dark space with few other visible details. Then we see a hand go up with a gun and shoot Archer in the chest. That hand extends straight out in front of the camera and thus places the spectator in the position of the murderer. The scene then cuts to a nighttime bedroom, barely illuminated. The phone rings. Spade sits up in bed, turns on a light, and answers the phone, only to find his partner Archer has been killed. The framing of this moment is masterful. Bogart remains at the edge of the frame throughout the entire scene. Dead center, but at the very top of the frame, is the lamp he turned on. Hanging from above, it casts harsh light down the center of the frame but does little to illuminate Spade off to the side. Instead, it illuminates a clock that is dead center of the frame, facing forward, on the bedside table. At the time, this was an unusual framing of a Hollywood superstar. There's none of the traditional high-key, low-contrast lighting of the actor—dead center and flooded in light, an all-good protagonist with a warm glow about him. Instead, the audience is shown a man in profile, partly in the shadow and, indeed, a partly shady character. One can't help but wonder if the frame is composed the way it is as a joke, as if Huston is saying, "Look what is in the center of the frame and flooded with light—it's the clock. It's time for a new way of shooting and lighting these actors. It's time for a new visual narrative style, one that corresponds to hard-boiled detective fiction, where the protagonist is so appealing specifically because he is shady, because he is off-center and you never understand his character fully." Between Huston's addition of a scene that placed the spectator in the position of the killer and his careful framing of Spade, he creates the noir vision the era calls for, where there are no perfect heroes and none of us has clean hands.

SC

Episode 5 || 08/15/05

Noireme 025: *Chinatown* (1974)

N = 00:09:26 ‖ RT = 02:10:25 ‖ RTP = 07.233%

N = 00:09:55

In *Chinatown,* Roman Polanski uses a self-conscious visual design to teach the audience how to look, where to look, and the stakes of looking. There is an early masking shot through a pair of binoculars where Polanski adds a little wiggle to imply we are seeing through the eyes of Jake Gittes (Jack Nicholson). Soon thereafter, we get another shot where we are tailing the same person, Hollis Mulwray (Darrell Zwerling). As Gittes watches the character in the side view mirror of his car, we are aware that we, too, are watching through a mirror. Finally, there is a shot—when Gittes goes to get photographic proof of Hollis Mulwray and his supposed affair—through the lens of a Leica camera. We watch the action in a medium close-up as Gittes holds the camera, and then the image Gittes would see through that camera plays in the camera. All these shots tell us this is a film about looking, but we are never going to be able to trust what we see.

RE

This is also a successful way to imply first-person subjectivity. Other filmic attempts had been made to imply that subjectivity, but they had failed. For example, there was the adaptation of *The Lady in the Lake,* where the whole film was shot from the first person and we only saw the protagonist at a moment when he closed the mirror on a medicine cabinet as he was shaving. That was too extreme. An audience likes to have a protagonist whom they see leading them into scenes, rather than stepping through that protagonist's point of view into scenes. And yet, shots like these successfully split the difference, giving us Jake Gittes's point of view without miring us in it.

SC
Episode 24 || 05/31/06

Noireme 026: *The Killing* (1956)

N = 00:06:39 || RT = 01:25:09 || RTP = 07.810%

The voice-over in *The Killing* is obsessively objective and omniscient, and differs from the subjective and limited first-person narration more common in hard-boiled detective fiction and film noir. The narrator seems to be an almost godlike entity—an objective voice who can see, and even anticipate, the entire unfolding of the narrative action. This objective narrative voice is contrasted with the limited point of view of Johnny Clay (Sterling Hayden) and his inability to see the big picture. I sometimes wonder if the game isn't fixed from the very start within Stanley Kubrick's universe in *The Killing*.

RE

I would say it is. As you stated, such an omniscient voice is unusual in film noir and hard-boiled fiction. Here we have a voice that knows everything from the beginning. As the movie starts and the voice-over begins, it trips us up, makes us wonder who we are hearing and how he knows—like a director would—how all of the pieces are going to fit together. The voice introduces Johnny Clay in this way: "About 7:00 p.m. that day, Johnny Clay, perhaps the most important thread in that unfinished fabric, furthered its design." This is an exceedingly strange way to introduce a character—first of all to say, and show, that the criminal mastermind and principal protagonist is but one thread in an "unfinished fabric," but also to suggest this is quite a yarn being spun. Who is the master pushing the shuttle through the loom? Who is it that's pulling all these threads into one narrative design?

SC
Episode 19 || 03/15/06

Noireme 027: *Good Night, and Good Luck* (2005)

N = 00:08:25 || RT = 01:32:48 || RTP = 09.070%

In George Clooney's *Good Night, and Good Luck,* there are several tribute shots to Hollywood film history and to television history that ultimately reveal something about noir. There is an early scene in the film when Fred Friendly (Clooney) and Edward R. Murrow (David Strathairn) watch newsreel footage of Joseph McCarthy. The shot comes directly out of Orson Welles's *Citizen Kane:* it's literally the same composition Welles uses at the beginning of *Kane* when characters in that film screen *March of Times* newsreels. In other words, Clooney is staging a knowing nod to *Citizen Kane* as another great film about journalism. Throughout the film, Clooney stages such tributes to Hollywood film history and to journalistic history. *Good Night, and Good Luck* is shot in black and white not out of nostalgia for the fifties but in order to historically reposition us as spectators. Edward R. Murrow came into America's living rooms in "See It Now" through the black-and-white screens of television. Likewise, this film is very knowledgeable in the way it cuts up historic footage with new footage shot by Clooney. The footage of Milo Radulovich or of Joseph McCarthy comes from original newsreels and gives the film a taste of historical authenticity. And while none of these choices makes this a film noir per se, such choices do make us recognize that noir and television were among the only media that dealt directly with the stories that defined American culture at that time: fears of communism and the atomic bomb in the 1950s created a culture of guilt and paranoia that noir and television were ideally positioned to portray (and exploit).

RE
Episode 22 || 05/01/06

Noireme 028: *The Hitch-Hiker* (1953)

N = 00:06:32 ‖ RT = 01:10:43 ‖ RTP = 09.239%

N = 00:07:24

The *Hitch-Hiker* introduces its psychotic killer very theatrically but in a way that also works thematically. After two men on vacation pick up an escaped convict, Emmett Myers (William Talman), he takes his place in the back-seat. Myers's face is initially shrouded in shadow. The first time we ever see his features is when he leans forward in the back seat and cinematographer Nicholas Musuraca strikes a high-key light to illuminate his face (a technique also used in *The Third Man*). At this moment, Myers's face pops up between the other two men (Frank Lovejoy on the left and Edmond O'Brien on the right), and he is shown to be the wedge between these two best friends. He is almost always staged between them—the axis of greatest change, the loose cannon, the random element, and an embodiment of psychotic madness that threatens to tear their lives apart.

RE
Episode 7 || 09/15/05

Noireme 029: *Batman Begins* (2005)

N = 00:13:26 || RT = 02:19:52 || RTP = 09.604%

N = 01:14:32

Christopher Nolan, one of our most assured contemporary noir filmmakers, offers up in the visual design for *Batman Begins* a noir cityscape that recalls an important aesthetic antecedent for film noir. Gotham City (as a prototypical "dark city") is reimagined by Nolan and by his art direction and production personnel as a city that takes many of its design principles from German expressionism. This is a city that seems to come straight out of Fritz Lang's *Metropolis*.

RE

Initially, that's true. The beginning of the film, when Wayne Sr. (Linus Roache) is still alive, features a sunbathed futuristic vision that looks like something Lang would have created. That quickly deteriorates, and when this becomes a dark city, it seems to cast an eye to a famous neo-noir cityscape—to wit, that in *Blade Runner*. There are images in *Batman Begins* when the crooked cop is walking through the streets, the rain is dumping, and we have all of these strange and unexplained influences of Asian culture where we feel we are on the set of *Blade Runner*.

SC
Episode 3 || 07/15/05

Noireme 030: *The Grifters* (1990)

N = 00:10:49 || RT = 01:50:19 || RTP = 09.805%

Roy Dillon (John Cusack) holds his stomach right after being hit with a club by a bartender who caught him on the grift. This detail comes straight out of the source material, Jim Thompson's 1963 novel *The Grifters,* which begins like this: "As Roy Dillon stumbled out of the shop, his face was a sickish green, and each breath he drew was an incredible agony. A hard blow in the guts can do that to a man, and Dillon had gotten a hard one. Not with a fist, which would have been bad enough, but from the butt-end of a heavy club." From the outset and throughout its duration, *The Grifters* is true to its hard-boiled literary source material, and many of its strengths as a film are born of Thompson's strengths as a writer.

RE
Episode 16 || 02/01/06

Noireme 031: *Blade Runner* (1982)

N = 00:11:20 ‖ RT = 01:56:27 ‖ RTP = 10.169%

N = 00:26:49

Blade Runner can be seen as the visual template for most contemporary tech noir and science fiction noir films. Its look has been widely imitated in other films. Director Ridley Scott has discussed in interviews how he came up with *Blade Runner*'s visual design. Scott set the film forty years in the future but also made it look as if it could have been happening forty years in the past. When *Blade Runner* was released in 1982, forty years earlier would have placed the film into the classic era of film noir. The visual dichotomies of the past and the future heighten the film's visual power. Ridley Scott's futuristic, postmodern, and Asian-influenced Los Angeles merges with an urban architecture that appears as if it were taken straight out of a black-and-white Jacob Riis photograph of New York City from the 1940s. Film noir is constantly coming "out of the past," such that even our visions of the future draw upon our noir models of the past.

RE
Episode 6 || 09/01/05

Noireme 032: *The Maltese Falcon* (1941)

N = 00:10:42 || RT = 01:40:29 || RTP = 10.649%

N = 00:12:18

There's an early scene in *The Maltese Falcon* that abandons traditional framing and creates a template for the subjective camera work of noir. Spade (Bogart) returns to his apartment and two detectives come to question him on where he has been that evening. The camera remains relatively stable in this scene, panning, tilting, and tracking only slightly. But the actors are constantly in motion. As they move around the room, nearer to or farther from the camera, they seem to change in size. We realize Huston is doing something with the staging that reflects what is happening in the narrative, that is, he is showing us that somebody has the upper hand at any moment in the dialogue. We can't even say at the end of this scene which of the actors is the tallest: the biggest character is the one who has the upper hand at any given moment. At one moment, Bogart seems to tower over the others; then the two detectives seem to tower over him.

SC

This scene is a gem of visual economy and narrative-driven compositions. In this particular scene, we can see one of John Huston's gifts as a visual storyteller. Huston doesn't fool the audience by keeping things out of sight, but rather he shows us things in plain sight.

RE
Episode 5 || 08/15/05

Noireme 033: *Double Indemnity* (1944)

N = 00:12:55 ‖ RT = 01:47:32 ‖ RTP = 12.012%

PHYLLIS: Mr. Neff, why don't you drop by tomorrow evening about eight-thirty. He'll be in then.

WALTER: Who?

PHYLLIS: My husband. You were anxious to talk to him weren't you?

WALTER: Yeah, I was, but I'm sort of getting over the idea, if you know what I mean.

PHYLLIS: There's a speed limit in this state, Mr. Neff. Forty-five miles an hour.

WALTER: How fast was I going, officer?

PHYLLIS: I'd say around ninety.

WALTER: Suppose you get down off your motorcycle and give me a ticket.

PHYLLIS: Suppose I let you off with a warning this time.

WALTER: Suppose it doesn't take.

PHYLLIS: Suppose I have to whack you over the knuckles.

WALTER: Suppose I bust out crying and put my head on your shoulder.

PHYLLIS: Suppose you try putting it on my husband's shoulder.

WALTER: That tears it.

In *Double Indemnity,* the characters often say one thing as the director shows another. The film is a great example of how writers crafted their words carefully to get past censorship in the era of the production code, but directors and actors nonetheless took those words and made them ripe with nuance on screen. The script of *Double Indemnity* is, on the surface, largely innocuous. For example, Walter Neff (Fred MacMurray) and Phyllis Deitrichson (Barbara Stanwyck) can have a conversation without saying anything too racy, but the whole thing is loaded with innuendo. When we watch them deliver this type of dialogue on the screen, the words combine with the way they are looking at each other, the way they are lit. These are not only verbal double entendres but also visual double entendres.

RE
Episode 2 || 07/08/05

Noireme 034: *The Killers* (1946)

N = 00:12:27 ‖ RT = 01:52:04 ‖ RTP = 12.127%

Near the beginning of *The Killers*, Nick (Phil Brown) runs to tell "The Swede" (Burt Lancaster) two men are coming to kill him. "The Swede" replies, "I'm through with . . . running around." What we see at play in this exchange is the fundamental question of the postwar era—the question Camus poses in his 1940 essay *The Myth of Sisyphus*: "There is but one truly serious philosophical problem, and that is suicide. Judging whether life is or is not worth living amounts to answering the fundamental question of philosophy" (Camus 1991, 3). In the Hemingway source story for *The Killers*, the only physical detail we have for "The Swede" is that he has a mashed-up face. In the film, as he is gunned down and lays dying in his bed, he reaches up with his right hand to grasp the bed frame, and what we see is a prominent scar on his hand. This is a very different sort of scar, because it doesn't indicate that he has taken a beating. It would seem to indicate that he has given a beating, that he has gone down fighting; and yet, he doesn't go down fighting. *The Killers* examines the story behind the scar "The Swede" bears; it is the story of the reasons for his decision not to fight any longer.

SC

This is the question raised by the myth of Sisyphus: the story of a man doomed for all eternity to roll a rock up a hill without ever completing his task. Camus and Siodmak both pay attention to the instant at which Sisyphus decides to go back down the hill to get started over again—or, in "The Swede's" case, decides not to.

RE

This is the key part of Camus's argument. The *absurde* allows us to recognize, in the words of Camus, that "by solitary effort . . . and in that day-to-day revolt he [Sisyphus] gives proof of his only truth, which is defiance" (Camus 1991, 55). And so it's at the moment that Sisyphus turns and looks back down at the rock that has crashed to the plains below, and decides to take that first step back down to retrieve it, that he becomes greater than his fate. With this action, fate itself is, to some degree, undermined. But "The Swede" finally gets to a point where he's just too tired to take that step.

SC

Episode 10 || 11/01/05

Noireme 035: *The Grifters* (1990)

N = 00:14:44 ‖ RT = 01:50:19 ‖ RTP = 13.355%

SMACK

The Grifters goes to great lengths to show us the working life of a grifter —something that takes a lot of practice and a great deal of skill. There is a scene where Roy Dillon (John Cusack) is laying in bed flipping a coin. As he puts the coin on the back of his hand, he says, "Smack!" then tries to guess whether it's heads or tails. The scene shows Roy's craft as a grifter. He is always fighting against the law of averages. When scamming people, when doing something illicit, sooner or later the law of averages is going to catch up to you. Roy Dillon is trying to cheat the probabilities of a coin flip, but the flip of a coin is always a fifty-fifty proposition. Roy believes he can get a grifter edge by just flipping *enough* coins—that he may actually grift fate itself.

RE
Episode 16 || 02/01/06

Noireme 036: *The Big Sleep* (1946)

N = 00:15:53 ‖ RT = 01:53:51 ‖ RTP = 13.951%

The Big Sleep is frequently at its best when it stays closest to Raymond Chandler's novel, as evidenced early in the film when Philip Marlowe (Humphrey Bogart) pretends that he's a fey book collector. He adopts the offbeat persona to investigate A. J. Geiger's bookstore (really a front for pornography), searching for a possible lead in his case. Marlowe upturns the bill of his cap, puts his sunglasses on the edge of his nose, and talks in a slightly high-pitched mousy voice, trying to put one over on the bookstore's one employee (Dorothy Malone). When we see the performance, we realize Bogart's comedic abilities were underused in most of his noir roles. He seems to enjoy these scenes and continues the playful and sexualized masquerade (though this time heterosexual) in ways that now exceed the source material when he goes across the street to another bookseller. That scene is filled with double entendres and implied lovemaking that Bogart delivers with talent and obvious relish.

RE
Episode 11 || 11/15/05

Noireme 037: *The Postman Always Rings Twice* (1946)

N = 00:15:58 || RT = 01:52:50 || RTP = 14.151%

N = 00:21:58

The Postman Always Rings Twice dives deep into the metaphoric resonances of its locales—often using them against their established tropological values. Frank Chambers (John Garfield) and Cora Smith's (Lana Turner) nighttime beach rendezvous uses the ocean to suggest a barrier to their relationship. Rather than opening up possibilities for these two characters, the ocean seems to be an absolute limit to any westward expansion fantasy of progress or forward motion. The ocean's a dead end, as confirmed at the end of the film when Cora goes out for her fateful swim. Likewise, the film undermines the trope of the open road as Frank and Cora try to make their getaway. The road and its earthiness are no escape either but rather another metaphor of how "stuck" these characters are. Metaphorically, they cannot escape by sea or land, and for Cora in particular there is no salvation. Despite her resplendent white outfits, she is dirty, as the road quickly reminds her (and us).

RE
Episode 30 || 12/01/06

Noireme 038: *Laura* (1944)

N = 00:12:55 ‖ RT = 01:27:07 ‖ RTP = 14.827%

The atmosphere of a given movie might best be described as the physical sensation one gets from watching it, and physical sensations come from set dressing and décor as well as from the cinematography and the score. *Laura* is a very atmospheric noir, dominated by a single painting. Throughout the film, the painting looms in the background, frequently decentered—a kind of "ghost character," which reminds the characters in the film and the audience in the theater of the absent presence of Laura. Director Otto Preminger frequently stages actors in the foreground and the middle ground exchanging pieces of acting business and dialogue as the painting hangs in the background. Then, in one of film noir's most sublime uses of set dressing, Laura "comes back to life"—the camera panning from the painting on the wall to a flesh and blood Laura (Gene Tierney)—revealing just how hung up Detective Mark McPherson (Dana Andrews) has been on her idealized image.

RE
Episode 9 || 10/14/05

Noireme 039: *Touch of Evil* (1958)

N = 00:18:53 || RT = 01:50:41 || RTP = 17.061%

Marlene Dietrich plays with her star persona in *Touch of Evil* as the character of a Madam who embodies the lost glamour and lost innocence of prewar Hollywood. We are first introduced to her character when she utters the line "we're closed." This line—perfectly delivered by one of the *grandes dames* of Hollywood—resonates with extranarrative meaning. "The Hollywood that Orson Welles and I knew around 1941, around the time of *Citizen Kane* is 'closed,'" she seems to be saying. Toward the end of the film, she has another line that functions in a similar manner. Tanya (Dietrich) looks at Quinlan (Welles) and says, "Your future is all used up." These two lines carry extradiegetic meaning: Orson Welles is trapped between a past that is closed and a future that is used up. *Touch of Evil* retrospectively marks a turning point for Welles. He is already done as a major director in Hollywood. After this film, Welles will mostly work on unrealized film projects and smaller films made in Europe. Welles lives for almost thirty years after *Touch of Evil* and was still in his prime as a filmmaker. But Welles sensed he was never going to get the reins to make another American movie and played out that drama poignantly in *Touch of Evil*.

RE
Episode 31 || 01/01/07

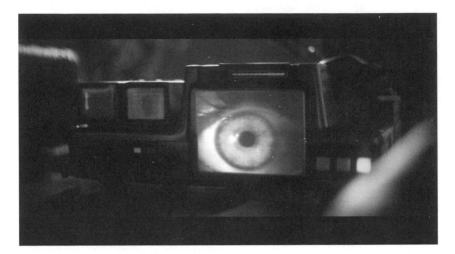

Noireme 040: *Blade Runner* (1982)

N = 00:21:26 ‖ RT = 01:56:27 ‖ RTP = 18.406%

N = 00:21:51

In the film *Blade Runner,* "Blade Runners" are the cops whose job it is to hunt down humanoid replicants that have escaped. Blade Runners usually identify replicants using a special machine that focuses on the eye in order to detect involuntary responses of the retina. Through a series of very personal questions, they can elicit signs of inappropriate emotional responses in replicants, born of their incomplete internal moral code. Ultimately, that's what gives the replicants away. But of course, the same thing could be said of noir protagonists. They, too, have an incomplete internal moral code and thus have inappropriate moral responses. And so often the clue that a noir protagonist has gone astray is in the eyes; think of the great scene between Fred MacMurray and Barbara Stanwyck in *Double Indemnity,* when at the very end he gets close and looks in her eyes, and she realizes, just before he shoots her, that something has gone awry.

SC
Episode 6 || 09/01/05

Noireme 041: *He Walked by Night* (1948)

N = 00:15:07 ‖ RT = 01:19:03 ‖ RTP = 19.123%

N = 00:16:03

A WAR OF PROCEDURES

He Walked by Night is a "ripped from the headlines" B film based on the real-life villainy of Irwin Walker, represented by the character of Roy Morgan (Richard Basehart). Drawing on actual case files, *He Walked by Night* is a semi-documentary police procedural that foregrounds new law enforcement technologies in the postwar period. There is the sense that, through these means, the police could still contain such villainy.

RE

Here we are shown procedures in detail, which creates a sense of security and conveys the message that the police can contain even the most diabolical and intelligent villain. But ultimately this is a procedural not only because it shows police work but also because it is a story of the war of two procedures. We see how methodical Roy Morgan is in his execution of these crimes: how he changes the license plates on his car, how he constantly changes his method and his appearance, and that he has great facility with electronics because of his time as a radio dispatcher in the war. Thus, he is able to listen in on police broadcasts and is able to deduce the methods they are using to try to track him down. What do the police have at their disposal? They have their radios, but they also have databases where they can run serial numbers. They have personnel at their disposal so they can cast a dragnet, and even though it comes up empty initially, eventually their sheer numbers make the difference. They have an advanced ballistics laboratory, where actor Jack Webb is the lab technician—a different role from the detective he will play in *Dragnet*. They comb through files (files upon files) for patterns of criminal activity—their "modus operandi" files. Plus, they have access to the files of others: the war department, other police departments, the post office, and other government organizations. Finally, they have forensic artists who can build up images of the criminal's face as scant details come to light. Their procedure—monotonous and relentlessness—eventually prevails. The combined weight of these things is too great for Morgan.

SC

Episode 25 || 06/14/06

Noireme 042: *Kiss Me Deadly* (1955)

N = 00:20:20 ‖ RT = 01:46:02 ‖ RTP = 19.176%

Kiss Me Deadly is shot in a deep focus style. This is not typical of films noir, which so often use lighting tricks and shallow depth of field to hide limited décor and cheap set dressing. Here, cinematographer Ernest Laszlo's beautiful lensing allows the audience to see from the foreground to the background plane with great visual clarity. A deep focus style makes sense in terms of this film's historical context. In the mid-1950s, Hollywood was responding to the challenge from television in a variety of ways—with widescreen aspect ratios like CinemaScope, with color and stereo sound, and with bigger budgets to tell epic stories. Films noir in particular encountered challenges from television because these films were rarely big budget or Technicolor affairs, and police procedurals like *Dragnet* were playing nearly every night of the week on TV. But noir films could signal their difference from the look and design of 1950s television through techniques such as location shooting and complicated camera techniques. One of the pleasures of watching *Kiss Me Deadly* is the tension between its absurdly simple story and its absurdly complicated depth of field.

RE
Episode 32 || 02/01/07

Noireme 043: *The Asphalt Jungle* (1950)

N = 00:23:11 ‖ RT = 01:52:04 ‖ RTP = 20.687%

As many great acting turns as there are in *The Asphalt Jungle,* perhaps the two greatest come from Sterling Hayden as Dix Handley and Marc Lawrence as Cobby. They are a fascinating juxtaposition, the one seeming to embody a sort of steadfast simplicity of the country (Dix) and the other the seductive savvy of the city (Cobby)—the unshakeable, unflappable rural type pitted against the fast-talking, fast-thinking, money-up-front urbanite. But ultimately the tensions born of their contrasting characters are also present in the person of Marilyn Monroe. Her screen time is limited to just a few minutes, yet she seems to embody, all by herself, this same mix of rural simplicity and urban seductive savvy—of tremendous innocence and scorching sexual appeal that is potentially explosive (the very mix to which Americans always seem fatally attracted). She is Norma Jean.

SC
Episode 8 || 10/01/05

Noireme 044: *The Big Sleep* (1946)

N = 00:23:35 || RT = 01:53:51 || RTP = 20.714%

When we watch *The Big Sleep,* we see why Bogart is *the* screen Marlowe. He manages to convey Marlowe's rumination, and that is never easy for an actor to do. In Chandler's novels, we often have a scene that lets us know that Marlowe's working through a problem; usually, we see him go to his chess board and work through a series of moves, or his character thinks or talks about working through chess moves. This lets us know he is working through a case, and it's hard mental work. What does Bogart do to short-hand such scenes? A simple gesture. Over and over in this film when he is reasoning something through, he rubs his right ear. It's a great touch and a sign of Bogart's genius. He once said, "I'm an actor. I just do what comes naturally," and that seems to be true here. We don't even have the sense he's doing it consciously. Instead, we get the sense that he's simply embodying the character, that it's something the character would do. Bogart lent Chandler's creation a realism, weight, and gravity that no other interpretation of Marlowe ever matched.

SC
Episode 11 || 11/15/05

NOIREME 045: *RIFIFI* (1955)

N = 00:24:36 ‖ RT = 01:58:35 ‖ RTP = 20.745%

Despite its reputation as an American film style, noir owes a great deal to German émigré directors: Fritz Lang, Robert Siodmak, and Otto Preminger came over to America with a European sensibility and changed the way Hollywood told hard-boiled stories. In the making of *Rififi,* we get the reverse trajectory—a Hollywood filmmaker, Jules Dassin, working in France due to the blacklist in the United States, bringing with him the American attitude, in order to make an American-style, hard-boiled film within the French film industry. The result is a film full of luscious collisions.

RE

There's no greater such collision than a scene in a nightclub when Viviane (Magali Noël), the club's singer, performs a song that explains what "rififi" means. As she's singing, there's a screen in the background onto which is projected an image of a cobblestone street, and behind the screen is a man in a suit and a hat with a cigarette in his mouth, dancing an interpretive dance that acts out the lyrics of her song. It's hard to imagine an American noir would ever contain a scene—and it's a crucial scene to the film—with an interpretive dance that acts out a definition of a slang term that is the title of the film. A truly luscious collision, and the highly stylized vision of noir that will prove crucial to French crime directors such as Jean-Luc Godard. Indeed, it's hard to imagine *Breathless* without a precedent like Jules Dassin's *Rififi.*

SC
Episode 12 || 12/01/05

Noireme 046: *The Man Who Wasn't There* (2001)

N = 00:25:06 ‖ RT = 01:55:48 ‖ RTP = 21.675%

N = 01:08:16

There are two shots in the Coens' *The Man Who Wasn't There* that demonstrate how the film repeats visual motifs that tend to confuse rather than clarify. In the first of these shots, Ed Crane (Billy Bob Thornton) is on the mezzanine of the department store owned by his wife's lover, a nether space between the party going on downstairs and the offices upstairs. We see a space of light off to the upper left of the frame, spilling down the staircase from up above (a staircase whose ascent appears barred by a foreground obstruction), and dim light to either side coming up over the balcony. Ed is just left of center walking toward the camera, but is entirely in shadow. Behind him, there is a space that is almost impossible to understand—a pyramid shape, with a hard, diagonal line to either side of Ed and little lines coming down behind him with some sort of object hanging at their bottom. While early scenes were replete with clean, right angles, at this moment things shift toward diagonals and we wonder if this shift corresponds to things spinning out of control for Ed. This composition occurs again when lawyer Freddy Riedenschneider (Tony Shalhoub) is in the jail cell with Ed and his wife Doris (Frances McDormand). Riedenschneider is spinning out a possible defense for Doris, who faces a murder rap, talking about "some guy in Germany, named Fritz or Werner or something" who has a theory that the closer you look at things the less you're going to understand them. The scene opens with Riedenschneider facing away from the camera, just right of center in a triangle of light almost identical to the triangle of shadows that framed Ed earlier. What were vertical lines of something like a pendulum behind Ed are now shadows cast by the bars up in the window through which the light is pouring—an almost identical composition to, but the negative of, the original shot. We can't help but wonder what the Coens are up to, for these two shots are so obviously parallels of one another. They seem rife with meaning, and yet they frustrate any attempt to analyze what they mean.

SC
Episode 30 || 12/01/06

Noireme 047: *Good Night, and Good Luck* (2005)

N = 00:20:25 ‖ RT = 01:32:48 ‖ RTP = 22.001%

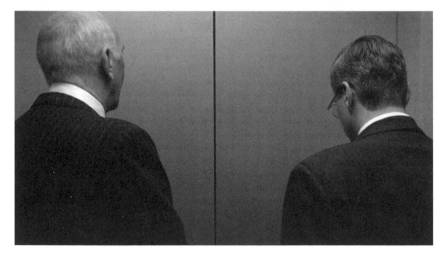

N = 00:52:57

Director George Clooney is very self-conscious about how he uses space in *Good Night, and Good Luck.* The film could easily have been a biopic about journalist Edward R. Murrow (David Strathairn), but Clooney decided to give us little information about Murrow. Instead, the film focuses on claustrophobic spaces in which the lead characters are trapped, where they cannot escape the pressure of their decision to confront Joseph McCarthy. Tight shots in elevators, the caged atmosphere of the news studio—Clooney shows us a world that is hermetically sealed. For its entire running length, this film rarely moves beyond a few broadcasting booths within the CBS building in New York. It is a world in which Edward R. Murrow and Fred Friendly (George Clooney) seem confined to go down to the studios or up to find their boss, CBS's chief executive William Paley (Frank Langella). In these repeated scenes, the elevator is a motif for exploring the pressure that is closing in, and the tension between characters mounts in that enclosed, suffocating space.

RE
Episode 22 || 05/01/06

Noireme 048: *Gun Crazy* (1950)

N = 00:19:30 ‖ RT = 01:27:01 ‖ RTP = 22.417%

N = 00:20:27

Many contemporary readings of films like *Gun Crazy* seem based on the film's current cult status. We read the film in relationship to its influence on other filmmakers and not necessarily in terms of the film itself. This leads us to ask what there is about *Gun Crazy*—the film itself—that would explain why it is so revered? Why do directors as diverse as Jean-Luc Godard (who cites this as one of his influences on *Breathless*) and Martin Scorsese (who says this had a huge impact on the way he approached directing films) love this film? It has some justifiably well-known and influential sequences, such as the four-minute-long-take from the backseat of the getaway car during the first heist sequence. So, while for much of its running time this film is quite ordinary, it is fondly remembered, even revered, for its "ecstatic" scenes. When the characters of Bart (John Dall) and Annie (Peggy Cummins) meet, it is one of the great, electrically charged "first dates" in the history of Hollywood cinema. There is no better symbol of the mating ritual than two people shooting matches off the top of each other's heads, with guns at point blank range.

RE
Episode 17 || 02/15/06

Noireme 049: *The Killers* (1946)

N = 00:23:26 || RT = 01:52:04 || RTP = 22.825%

The lead protagonist in *The Killers,* Jim Reardon (Edmond O'Brien), is an insurance company investigator, just like Barton Keyes (Edward G. Robinson) in *Double Indemnity.* In both cases, the lead investigator is not a law enforcement official but rather an insurance company employee who continues to stay on a case for the recovery of something that seems somewhat inconsequential in each of these stories—the insurance company's money. Then again, it's the money that motivates other characters in these films to undertake a series of double crosses that ultimately seal their fate.

RE

We have argued elsewhere that *The Killers* is an existentialist narrative, and in the existential world, free will has displaced God as the epistemological foundation of existence. In this context, it's interesting that O'Brien's character is in insurance because the way free will is expressed in America in the postwar period is as free enterprise. He is at once a detective who wants to get at the true lives people lived and someone who wants to get at the money those lives represent—but he refuses to accept that lives have only financial value.

SC

In the end, there is a merciless message in this film. All of the major plot threads are resolved and everyone gets what that have coming to them, but for what? All the reward that O'Brien gets for going through all of these machinations, for finding all the truth about "The Swede" and the femme fatale, and for understanding the murders and where the money is, is to return to the home office, announce the truth, and learn that the stockholders of the insurance company are going to save one-tenth of a cent in 1947.

RE

That may be Robert Siodmak's most biting commentary and one of the most bitter truths expressed by any postwar noir. Siodmak seems to say that in the postwar world we all bear "The Swede's" scar together; we all have to decide if we're going to fight with a broken hand or cash it in. And if in the end the only reward is financial remuneration, then we're in trouble.

SC
Episode 10 || 11/01/05

Noireme 050: *Sunset Blvd.* (1950)

N = 00:25:18 ‖ RT = 01:50:12 ‖ RTP = 22.958%

N = 00:28:00

In *Sunset Blvd.*, Joe Gillis's (William Holden) movement through locations visually signals the progression of his doom. He starts in a little one-room apartment, pounding out stories, and although it is a shabby existence, it's clearly one that is all his own. Later, he is brought to an equally shabby space, the space of the apartment above the garage at Norma Desmond's (Gloria Swanson) house, and we see he is no longer free. The shot that introduces Gillis into that apartment is one of the great subtle shots in noir history. When Max (Erich von Stroheim) walks Gillis into that apartment for the first time and flicks on the lights, there is an inexplicable shadow cast upon the wall. In fact, we can't tell if it is actually a shadow or a stain on the wallpaper of this rundown apartment, but it is in the shape of a noose—a straight vertical line with a loop at the bottom. It's easy to miss, but when Gillis enters that space, the first place he stands is with that noose right by his neck. We realize that the instant he takes Desmond's offer of a space that is part of her world, he is hanged. That night he has a nightmare that there is an organ grinder's monkey playing music. He wakes up the next morning in that apartment, and there actually is an organ playing from the mansion. At this moment, he is framed against the headboard of the bed—an iron bed whose bars spread out at the bottom and become tighter at the top; it looks like there is a net cast about his head. These subtle touches make us realize that, from the second Gillis enters Desmond's space, he is not going to get out alive.

SC
Episode 21 || 04/15/06

Noireme 051: *Murder, My Sweet* (1944)

N = 00:25:45 || RT = 01:46:02 || RTP = 24.285%

In my opinion, if you have to change the title of Raymond Chandler's source novel when adapting it to film so that moviegoers won't assume the man playing Marlowe is appearing in another of his popular musicals, you've cast the wrong man as Marlowe. Before playing the lead in *Murder, My Sweet,* Dick Powell's former film credits included *The Singing Marine, Cowboy from Brooklyn, Naughty but Nice, Happy Go Lucky,* and *Three Cheers for the Girls.* The Marlowe of literature had many talents—dogged determination, acid wit, a quick tongue, and a jaw that could take a shot—but crooning and dancing were never among them. However, the problem isn't simply one of what Powell did before *Murder, My Sweet;* it's more one of what he did with the role of Marlowe once landing it. Marlowe's gravity as a literary character is born of a substantial, existentialist weight. He is the sum of slow but seemingly inevitable action; watching him work is like watching a glacier advance. None of those things come through with Powell. He tries to be a chip off this block, and maybe he is a chip, but the heft of Marlowe's character is gone. Watching him work is more like watching someone ice skate. It's not lacking in a certain elegance, but it feels wholly unnatural for the part. A dance man who's bursting at the seams to be a dancer can never embody Marlowe. One moment, to me, really sums that up, and that's the moment when Powell plays hopscotch on the black-and-white checkerboard marble in the Grayle House. In fact, that's the moment when I lose all interest in Powell's portrayal of Marlowe. Marlowe would never play hopscotch in his clients' homes. This moment is so out of character for Marlowe that it brings to a head something else I'd been feeling since the beginning of this film, and that is that the wit of Powell's voice-over is simply too glib in its delivery. When I read Chandler's Marlowe, I can almost feel the heartbreak in his humor and the gravity of that heartbreak. That's lacking here. Powell seems like a happy-go-lucky guy. I actually enjoy this performance, when I stop thinking of Powell's character as Philip Marlowe. But each time the name Marlowe comes up it's jarring, because Powell feels so different from any manifestation or embodiment of Marlowe that I ever envisioned while reading Chandler.

SC

Episode 26 || 06/30/06

Noireme 052: *Murder, My Sweet* (1945)

N = 00:25:46 ‖ RT = 01:46:02 ‖ RTP = 24.301%

One of the reasons Dick Powell's performance of Philip Marlowe is so powerful is that Powell the performer is bursting at the seams to come out. Yet, he initially plays the role in a wooden manner—very much contained, not allowing himself any extraneous movement. I believe that, if he was really intending to dance on those tiles, he could have done an incredible job. So I see that same scene in parodic terms and believe he actually moves cavalierly through the house in an exaggerated sense of trying to be true to Marlowe. This is actually how Marlowe, if he were doing a stutter step, would probably move. Powell could have done it with much more grace and style. For me, this moment comes through the screen as very in keeping with the Marlowe of literature. Another thing that works for me is the Powell voice-over; I like his voice, and I think it has the right air of gravity. There's always going to be the difficulty of adaptation. When people read the novels, they're going to get their own particular view of a character. When you try to put a flesh and blood actor into the shoes of any character, there are going to be disagreements. Powell does have the proper amount of gravitas and captures the world-weariness essential to the Marlowe character.

RE
Episode 26 || 06/30/06

Noireme 053: *Out of the Past* (1947)

N = 00:23:45 || RT = 01:36:38 || RTP = 24.577%

N = 00:25:28

Shortly after Jeff Bailey (Robert Mitchum) and Kathie Moffat (Jane Greer) start to cultivate their relationship in *Out of the Past,* there is a scene that has them walking a lonely beach by moonlight. Their interactions are getting more and more intimate, and the visual barriers between them that we saw in earlier frames are being eliminated little by little. Here they are hand in hand—a picturesque scene with old, overturned fishing boats and fishing nets hung out to dry. At this moment, they finally start to level with one another about why he is in Mexico and why she is in Mexico. She admits she has run from Whit Sterling (Kirk Douglas); he admits having been hired by Sterling to track her down. As she tells her side of the story, she gets closer and closer, and becomes more and more seductive. Finally, she leans in and says, "You believe me, don't you Jeff?" In one of the most iconic of all noir lines, he looks at her and says, "Baby, I don't care." Not only is the writing pitch perfect, but as they kiss the camera moves in and we lose some of the background; all that's left behind them are the fishing nets, crisscrossing the background of the frame. So it is this kiss, this moment when Bailey decides to throw caution to the wind, that traps him. It's a wonderful visual metaphor and a scene that captures many of the fundamental characteristics of film noir. There is often a generally good guy who makes a bad decision out of desire or greed, or in many cases both. There is a savvy and usually seductive woman only too happy to help him make that decision. In this case, desire is clearly to blame, and at the moment Bailey makes his decision, he finds himself caught in Moffat's designs.

SC
Episode 1 || 07/02/05

Noireme 054: *Double Indemnity* (1944)

N = 00:28:28 || RT = 01:47:32 || RTP = 26.472%

There are many visual clues in *Double Indemnity* that are as subtle and stylized as the narrative. When Walter Neff (Fred MacMurray) finally decides he is going to go along with Phyllis Dietrichson's (Barbara Stanwyck) plot to harm her husband—that he is going, as an insurance investigator, to help her commit a crime to collect the insurance premium—director Billy Wilder gives us subtle and ironic cues that MacMurray is in trouble. Phyllis comes to his apartment, where he has been thinking through the setup. He opens the door to her, and at that moment she comes into the apartment wearing pants. Until this time, she had been dressed scantily—first in a towel, and then in a skirt. Now, at the moment she forces the action, she is suddenly wearing pants. In this scene, Wilder also chooses to film Neff in profile more often, and Dietrichson face forward—the classic framing of the male protagonist, the active player. These subtle clues show that she is now in charge; she is wearing the pants.

SC
Episode 2 || 07/08/05

Noireme 055: *The Killing* (1956)

N = 00:26:26 || RT = 01:25:09 || RTP = 31.043%

While the action of *The Killing* is focused primarily on the complications of a heist, the atmosphere and key aspects of the plot are dominated by the presence of one of the great femmes fatales in the history of film noir—Sherry, played to perfection by Marie Windsor. She manipulates her husband George (Elisha Cook Jr.), telling him that it's nice to have affection, but at a certain point it's not enough: "All you've ever done is talk about loving me. That's all I've had for the last five years is talk. Now that you have the chance to do something, buy me things . . ." And that's the end of the quote. Of course, George breaks; he can't stand the thought of not having Sherry's affection. It's a great scene not only because it shows the point at which things break down in the criminal plan but also because in juxtaposition with the very next scene it's a great pun. Director Stanley Kubrick cuts from that scene, where Sherry is working on George, to a scene where Sterling Hayden's character, Johnny Clay, is entering "The Academy of Chess and Checkers." The door might as well read "The Academy of Chumps and Suckers"; through her expert manipulation of George, Sherry is effectively playing the whole gang—even Clay, the man who thinks he's calling the moves.

SC

Episode 19 || 03/15/06

Noireme 056: *Sunset Blvd.* (1950)

N = 00:35:49 || RT = 01:50:12 || RTP = 32.501%

The automobile is a key motif in many Los Angeles–based films noir. Billy Wilder's *Double Indemnity* begins with a car careening out of control in the deserted, nighttime streets of L.A. That car helps introduce us to Walter Neff (Fred MacMurray) and suggests from the first frames that this is a story about "losing control." *Sunset Blvd.* fundamentally hinges on what might be one of the most mundane acts of fate ever: Joe Gillis (William Holden) is three months behind on his car payments, and he chooses the driveway of Norma Desmond (Gloria Swanson) to hide from the men trying to repossess his automobile. Ultimately, the repo men find Gillis's car, stranding him in the company of Desmond and sealing his fate. To have one's car repossessed might be the ultimate symbol of the loss of power in the city of Los Angeles.

RE

The motif of the automobile plays a crucial role at another moment in *Sunset Blvd.* as well. Norma Desmond receives a call from Paramount Studios and thinks that her career is being reborn, that she is going to get a chance to film the historical drama she's writing with Joe Gillis, and that Cecil B. DeMille will direct. When she goes to the lot, she learns that they only called because they thought her old car would be perfect for a period film they were making. In essence, the principal plot twists and psychological intrigues of *Sunset Blvd.* turn on two cars.

SC
Episode 21 || 04/15/06

Noireme 057: *The Hitch-Hiker* (1953)

N = 00:23:01 ‖ RT = 01:10:43 ‖ RTP = 32.548%

The Hitch-Hiker cleverly comments on the paranoia and claustrophobia of the era in which it was produced. Fugitive convict Emmett Myers (William Talman), the hitchhiker, has one defective eye that never quite closes, even when he's sleeping. Thus, as the film shows, the eye that is always watching is a defective, criminal eye. This is an especially interesting narrative device at the time of the Red Scare, when there was more oversight into American society in general, and Hollywood in particular, than ever before. In theory, Big Brother was watching to make sure things would go the way they needed to. But *The Hitch-Hiker* seems to suggest that the Big Brother who is watching is not the guy we want calling the shots.

SC
Episode 7 || 09/15/05

Noireme 058: *Chinatown* (1974)

N = 00:42:28 || RT = 02:10:25 || RTP = 32.562%

FLORSHEIM SHOE

How do you show what a character is thinking? Directors and screenwriters often use repetitive words as motifs that allow the audience to make linkages from scene to scene. In *Chinatown,* there are three moments of fragmented dialogue that represent the inner mental processes of Jake Gittes (Jack Nicholson). The first occurs in the scene when Gittes goes to the Mulwray residence and bumps into the Chinese gardener, who delivers the famous line "bad for the glass." It's a mispronunciation of the words "bad for the grass," and when that line is repeated later in the film by Gittes, we see how he, as a detective, starts to put the clues together. The next such instance is the line "Florsheim shoe," which Gittes repeats after having lost his shoe in a perilous incident. It draws attention to what he is focused on at that moment and again gives us a flash of insight into his style of ratiocination. The final instance surrounds the fragmented line "as little as possible," which Gittes says twice in the story. It comes out of a line about the kind of police work done in Chinatown ("as little as possible"), because there was no way to resolve problems there, and is delivered at Gittes's most world-weary moment in the film. Taken together, these lines seem to externalize Gittes's internal thoughts.

RE

Roman Polanski makes another analogous decision to complement these moments in the script, and that is to foreground small sounds. Elsewhere, we've discussed the desaturation of the color palette in *Chinatown.* Conversely, there is a saturation of sounds: when doors click shut or slide open; when phones ring; when bedsprings creak; and when the chauffeur at the Mulwray mansion is polishing the car and we hear the squeaking. They give us additional insights into the story and into characters' emotional states and inner thoughts but also serve to interrupt the rumination of Gittes. Each time that he's starting to see a pattern, starting to get the feel of something, one of these sounds interrupts his thinking.

SC
Episode 24 || 05/31/06

Noireme 059: *Gun Crazy* (1950)

N = 00:33:20 || RT = 01:27:01 || RTP = 38.307%

N = 00:36:05

Gun Crazy is replete with moments that might best be described as noir camp. The holdup scenes are prime examples—from the long-take robbery sequence carried out in campy cowboy outfits to the extensive footage of the last heist in a meat packing plant. But the first heist in the film already had an additional element of camp that might be easy to miss. When Bart Tare (John Dall) and Annie Starr (Peggy Cummins) do the holdup, in order to scare the teller into giving over the money, Bart shoots a gumball machine. And this image of shooting a bubble gum machine is both a literal act of violence and very metaphorically charged. It conveys the end of Bart Tare's bubblegum existence and signals that the rest of the film is going to have a much harder edge.

RE
Episode 17 || 02/15/06

Noireme 060: *The Asphalt Jungle* (1950)

N = 00:43:07 ‖ RT = 01:52:04 ‖ RTP = 38.474%

The Asphalt Jungle has a large ensemble cast. In the absence of one leading man—such as Humphrey Bogart, with whom John Huston had worked previously—everyone has the opportunity for more screen time, and everyone has the opportunity to shine. Sterling Hayden delivers a powerful performance as Dix Handley, the big thug, or "hooligan," in the film. Louis Calhern is smooth as oil as Alonzo Emmerich, the dirty lawyer who funds the operation. Jean Hagen breaks our heart with her steadfast devotion as Doll Conovan, the young lady who is hopelessly sweet on Dix. James Whitmore is profoundly tough as Gus, the handicapped getaway driver. Sam Jaffe delivers a nuanced and calculated but ultimately tragic Doc Erwin Riedenschneider, the mastermind criminal behind it all. Marc Lawrence plays Cobby Cobb, the small-time, fast-talking front man. Finally, Anthony Caruso is the unflappable box man, Louis Ciavelli. This cast works beautifully together, and Huston's assembly of this cast was crucial, just like the assembly of the right crew is important inside the narrative itself.

SC
Episode 8 || 10/01/05

Noireme 061: *Rififi* (1955)

N = 00:47:41 ‖ RT = 01:58:35 ‖ RTP = 40.211%

N = 00:48:10

Jules Dassin's 1955 *Du rififi chez les hommes* was the first picture he directed after being blacklisted in Hollywood in 1950, and in many ways the film seems to be an allegory of what he suffered because of HUAC (House Un-American Activities Committee). This film opens with Tony le Stéphanois (Jean Servais) fresh off a stint in prison, and he appears to be in poor health. In fact, he seems to be suffocating—coughing and sweating through early scenes of the movie as if he's struggling for air. It is only once this charming thief gets a job back—when he's back in his element and starting to rob things again—that he begins to breath easier and starts to look like a healthier individual. Tony orchestrates a complicated heist, which plays out in a nearly thirty-minute sequence with virtually no sound, at the very heart of the film. It opens with a first-person tracking shot, where the camera comes through the door into total darkness, a flashlight comes on, and the camera pans with the flashlight. We get the sense of being in the position of the intruder, breaking into this building. From this point, there's no dialogue. The heist is executed with gestures. Silence is important to building the suspense in the film, but it is also crucial to understanding this film in its historical context. Just a few years earlier, Dassin had been silenced in Hollywood and had to go overseas before being allowed to direct again (and it is probably no mistake that the character of Tony has just finished a five-year sentence—the very length of time Dassin suffered between directing *Night and the City* and *Rififi*). Tony assembles a foreign crew (who struggle to understand one another and communicate through gestures) who work with limited tools (their high-tech instruments are an umbrella and a fire extinguisher) in an attempt to pull off a complicated, coordinated effort in total silence. It's a brilliant microcosm of what Dassin had to go through as a director, in exile, and suggests that with this film Dassin has stolen back a little something of his own. At last he, like Tony, will breathe easier.

SC
Episode 12 || 12/01/05

Noireme 062: *Touch of Evil* (1958)

N = 00:45:36 || RT = 01:50:41 || RTP = 41.199%

N = 00:46:09

Touch of Evil is ultimately a cold-hearted film, not only in the story it is telling but in a larger sense as well; the film can be seen as a compilation of visual puns that unmask narrative filmmaking, that stage its demise, and ultimately Orson Welles offers viewers no alternative to this world of bleak, tongue-in-cheek self-referentiality. We could go so far as to argue that Welles is trying to steal the magic of cinema without giving us anything in exchange, as a scene right in the middle of the film suggests. Ramon Miguel Vargas (Charlton Heston) has left the scene of the interrogation to call his wife (Janet Leigh) at her hotel, and the action cuts back and forth from a store where Vargas is placing the call to Leigh's hotel room. Heston is framed in front of an unusual sign; because the store he is calling from belongs to a blind shopkeeper, the sign says, "If you are mean enough to steal from the blind, help yourself." The action cuts from Leigh's room, where we have just seen a speaker on the wall that looks just like a bulls-eye. We get the sense there is something vicious about this framing, like Welles is taking his best shot at filmmaking itself. It's as if he's stealing from us, the viewers—taking this shot at any casual viewer who isn't hip to what he's doing and ultimately laughing all the way to the bank.

SC
Episode 31 || 01/01/07

Noireme 063: *D.O.A.* (1950)

N = 00:34:26 ‖ RT = 01:23:32 ‖ RTP = 41.221%

N = 00:34:36

In *D.O.A.*, Frank Bigelow (Edmond O'Brien) hears that he has been poisoned and will not live much longer. He runs out of the doctor's office and goes on a mad dash through the streets of San Francisco, finally coming to rest in front of a newsstand. Behind him is a magazine rack with *Life* magazines on display, such that the word "life" repeats multiple times, surrounding Bigelow at a point when he doesn't have much of it left. What follows are two clichéd moments. First, a little girl stops in front of Bigelow, symbolizing innocence. Then a young couple greets one another, symbolizing romantic love. Director Rudolph Maté stages all of this to emphasize "loss"— the loss of life, innocence, and love.

RE

There is another, largely complimentary, way we could interpret these shots. We should note how the girl enters the scene. Her ball comes bouncing into the frame, and Bigelow bends down to pick it up and hand it back to her. She smiles and leaves. The next shot has a woman standing right next to Bigelow but not noticing him. Instead, she waves to her lover, who comes to greet her— all in silence before they walk off together. I think this progression suggests that the active man, whose purposeful action can make a difference, is gone. He has literally run himself ragged. After we see him wear himself out, the mise-en-scène shifts abruptly to make him the passive player; the ball comes to him, but at least the little girl is still willing to acknowledge his presence. Then, with the next shot of the young couple, the world forgets him completely. The action is happening right next to him, but it's as if he's not there. This could be read as Maté's take on what has happened in this postwar world. Not so long ago a man could make a difference with his action; now, suddenly, he is in a place where he's a passive part of the larger system, and he's quickly being forgotten. He is obsolete in the truest sense, for he is nearly out of circulation.

SC
Episode 27 || 09/01/06

Noireme 064: *On the Waterfront* (1954)

N = 00:45:12 ‖ RT = 01:47:35 ‖ RTP = 42.014%

N = 00:45:14

There's a telling moment in *On the Waterfront* when Elia Kazan gives the audience a sense of how the noir universe is often carved out of everyday existence. Terry Malloy (Marlon Brando) starts to romance Edie Doyle (Eva Marie Saint), sister of the guy whose murder at the hands of the mob Terry feels responsible for. While out together, they end up crashing a wedding reception at a little dockside bar, dancing closely in a dark and crowded space at the back. In the low-key lighting, it's easy to forget they are wedding crashers. Then all of a sudden, a light is flipped on, and the whole noir atmosphere is revealed for what it is—a lighting trick. This is not some dark corner of existence but rather a cheap, noisy wedding: the truth is both less menacing and less glamorous than it had seemed (as is often the case in the noir universe). In its juxtaposition with the previous moment, this simple flip of a light switch reveals the flipside of noir.

RE
Episode 23 || 05/15/06

Noireme 065: *Touch of Evil* (1958)

N = 00:47:55 ‖ RT = 01:50:41 ‖ RTP = 43.292%

As established in noiremes 007 ("Blowing Up Noir") and 062 ("Stealing from the Blind"), director Orson Welles stages self-reflexive puns in *Touch Of Evil* that ultimately constitute auto-exegesis; that is, they are narrative moments that reflect upon the narrative, visual moments that frame the act of film framing. One such pun plays out in the long scene in Manelo Sanchez's (Victor Millan) apartment when Hank Quinlan (Orson Welles) is accusing Sanchez of being the guy who has planted the bomb, while Quinlan himself is planting the evidence that's going to frame Sanchez. Initially, all of the players cast a single long shadow on the wall (typical of films noir). But from the moment the evidence is planted and then revealed (and we see there are two sticks of dynamite in Sanchez's apartment), if we look carefully we see the actors in the living room are now casting two shadows. It seems to be another of Welles's visual puns, with both a diegetic and extradiegetic meaning, this time on the idea of the "double cross." At the moment that the two sticks of dynamite are planted and found by the auteur of Sanchez's demise (also the auteur of the film), Welles blows open the noir mise-en-scène with this double entendre.

SC
Episode 31 || 01/01/07

Noireme 066: *The Maltese Falcon* (1941)

N = 00:43:51 || RT = 01:40:29 || RTP = 43.639%

A FLUTTER OF CURTAINS

There's a moment in *The Maltese Falcon* that shows the power of visual metonymy, demonstrating a method by which films noir could substitute an image of something banal but metaphorically charged for a narrative moment that could not be shown. Brigid O'Shaughnessy (Mary Astor) manages to seduce Sam Spade (Humphrey Bogart), who of course is very willing to be seduced. At the moment he leans over and kisses her, the camera pans to an open window with the curtains fluttering—at once a very subtle and not very subtle visual metaphor for the fact they're making love. This particular metonymic substitution comes up over and over again in film noir. In *Out of the Past,* at the moment that the Mitchum and Greer characters kiss and fall to the couch, the camera pans to the door and it bursts open to reveal a torrential rainstorm outside. It is a simple and visually charged method of deleting a love scene but hinting what has happened, and in the case of *The Maltese Falcon* we have to catch the hint. In a scene that follows shortly thereafter, O'Shaughnessy comes to Spade's office and calls him "darling," and they talk about loving one another. If we didn't catch the earlier hint that something profound happened between them, we might well wonder how they pass so quickly to loving one another.

SC
Episode 5 || 08/15/05

Noireme 067: *Murder, My Sweet* (1944)

N = 00:46:17 ‖ RT = 01:46:02 ‖ RTP = 43.650%

Near the middle of *Murder, My Sweet,* there is a drug-induced dream sequence that illustrates just what a masterful director Edward Dmytryk was. Philip Marlowe (Dick Powell) gets dragged by the wrongdoers to an alcohol and drug rehabilitation clinic (one of the shady "private sanitariums" of the day), and shot full of smack for a few of days—an attempt to find out what Marlowe really knows about a criminal event. He has crazy visions of the doctor chasing him, hypodermic needle in hand, as he goes through a series of increasingly smaller doorways. There are cobwebs over his vision and Dmytryk captures the scene with spinning cameras and moments that fade to blackness. This sequence is deeply suspenseful and visually inventive; it anticipates a more famous scene in Hitchcock's *Spellbound* by a year and allows us to see how far ahead of his time Dmytryk was.

SC

This scene in *Murder, My Sweet* also establishes a duality between the private investigator and the psychiatrist. They both run very similar types of businesses. They're trying to get inside the heads of their clients to find out things that even the clients may not fully understand. The radical subjectivity of *Murder, My Sweet* reminds us that the psyche of the private investigator is a horrible place to be. Though the ostensible purpose of this plot twist is to try to find out if Marlowe has the jade necklace, the pathos of the scene is played for the nightmare qualities of a detective who usually lives by his wits being "out of his wits."

RE

I think that insight helps us to understand one reason PI stories became so popular in the postwar years. So many people returned from the war psychologically scarred and were trying to work out "the case" of what it meant to live the life they were living, what the intrigue was that they were involved in. To be inside the head of a man who is scarred by the experience of having seen people killed is indeed a dark place to be.

SC
Episode 26 || 06/30/06

Noireme 068: *The Asphalt Jungle* (1950)

N = 00:52:00 ‖ RT = 01:52:04 ‖ RTP = 46.401%

N = 00:54:36

TIME AND CRIME

Time is a crucial element in the caper-heist film, a subgenre where there never seems to be enough of it. *The Asphalt Jungle* constantly reminds us, in very self-conscious ways, that time is running out for these characters and their objective. The heist sequence in particular is replete with shots of characters looking at clocks and watches. The proper management of time is crucial to the outcome of the heist: the ensemble cast of thieves has to operate like multiple watch movements in complete synchronicity. But time is always against them. Ultimately, caper-heist films are trapped in two concurrent temporal systems—one diegetic, one extradiegetic—that both work against the characters. Time is always running out on the characters during the heist, and on the film that tells their story.

RE
Episode 8 || 10/01/05

Noireme 069: *Touch of Evil* (1958)

N = 00:55:24 ‖ RT = 01:50:41 ‖ RTP = 50.053%

N = 00:55:33

In noiremes 007 ("Blowing Up Noir"), 062 ("Stealing from the Blind"), and 065 ("Doubled, Crossed"), we showed how director Orson Welles stages self-reflexive puns in *Touch of Evil* that ultimately constitute auto-exegesis, which is to say they are narrative moments that reflect upon the narrative and visual moments that frame the act of film framing; another such moment occurs at the very heart of the film — exactly the halfway point of its running time. Hank Quinlan (Orson Welles) has planted evidence in Manelo Sanchez's (Victor Millan) apartment. The scene cuts to outside the apartment, where Joe Grandi (Akim Tamiroff) and Quinlan are talking. Grandi is trying to convince Quinlan to do something illegal, as if planting evidence—as Quinlan just has—weren't enough. We see a shot of Quinlan's partner, Pete Menzies (Joseph Calleia), through a window as he stands inside a room across the street, looking out at Grandi and Quinlan talking. The room is divided between a light spot, where Menzies is positioned, and a spot of darkness that allows us to see a reflection on the windowpane of what is going on outside. It would be hard to stage a more self-reflexive shot than that— perfectly divided between the action of the "good" partner, bathed in light, who is watching, and the reflective side of the frame that captures (thanks to its inherent darkness) the reflection of Quinlan and Grandi as they speak outside, under the watchful eye of Menzies (and the audience). This split and mirrored framing is itself immediately mirrored in the next shot. The scene cuts to Janet Leigh's character (Susie Vargas) in the hotel. Initially, we are led to believe we're seeing a long shot of a landscape, but suddenly she lifts the shade on her hotel window and the landscape vanishes. We realize what we were seeing was the landscape reflected in the window of her room, but as the window fills with light we see her instead. These framings are clearly self-reflexive visual puns and demonstrate that this film is a masterpiece both as a narrative and as a self-reflexive commentary on that narrative.

SC

Episode 31 || 01/01/07

Noireme 070: *He Walked by Night* (1948)

N = 00:40:27 ‖ RT = 01:19:03 ‖ RTP = 51.170%

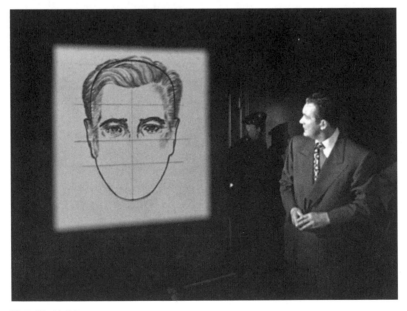

N = 00:42:24

There is a complex and very self-conscious *mise en abyme* in *He Walked by Night* that demonstrates how directors Alfred L. Werker and Anthony Mann were playing with cinematic conventions (a *mise en abyme* being series of frames within frames, where each framed image reproduces the image within which it is framed to create a "mirror" effect that recedes ad infinitum). That *mise en abyme* is the "build a picture of the man" scene at the heart of this film. It is the crowning moment of police procedure within this procedural, the device that makes the case. The officer who has been charged with finding Roy Morgan has an inspiration: why not create a series of police sketches? Some of the man's hairline, some of the eyes, some of his nose, some of his mouth, and some of his chin. Then these slides can be projected in a room full of people who have been victims of Roy Morgan's (Richard Basehart) holdups, and little by little, with their combined testimony, a picture of the man can be assembled. This scene starts with a shot of the projector in the foreground—the huge obstruction looming over the assembled audience—and in the background is the blank screen. Little by little, the victims sit in this dark screening room, projecting their memories onto this screen until a certain image is filled in, a certain story is told. It's hard to imagine a better metaphor for the cinematic process, or a mise-en-scène that could more aptly convey Werker and Mann's mastery of the medium and their understanding that a B film noir like *He Walked by Night* is an ideal forum for developing and demonstrating such mastery.

SC
Episode 25 || 06/14/06

Noireme 071: *On the Waterfront* (1954)

N = 00:57:02 ‖ RT = 01:47:35 ‖ RTP = 53.013%

N = 00:57:36

On the Waterfront makes manifest one of the dangers of film: something that is visually artful can make us forget how artless the message it conveys might be. At best, this film has a heavy-handed message even if it plays artfully on screen, and there is no doubt it does. It contains some of the most memorable scenes in film history: Terry alone in his pigeon coop; the famous "I could've been a contender" scene; or the conclusion of Father Barry's (Karl Malden) passionate speech to the longshoremen, as he is pulled up out of the cargo hold of the ship to a "higher plane." All of these moments are visually memorable, but taken together their message is not only heavy-handed but in many ways objectionable. Initially, it seems *On the Waterfront* stages Elia Kazan's self-doubt, and even self-loathing, over having acted as a stool pigeon during the HUAC hearings (indeed, the film opens with an accused stool pigeon being thrown from a rooftop). But as the film plays out, it becomes evident he is feeling no remorse. Instead, the people who squeal in this film are shown to be not only in the right but also, ultimately, righteous. If there is a moment in the dialogue that really sums that up, it's the moment when Father Barry is in the hold, standing over the body of the dead longshoreman who was "brave" enough to name names. He says, "Every time the mob puts the crusher on a good man, and tries to stop him from doing his duty as a citizen, it's a crucifixion. And anybody who sits around and lets it happen, keeps silent about something he knows has happened, shares the guilt of it just as much as the Roman soldier who pierced the flesh of our Lord." If that's not heavy-handed enough, the good father is then raised up, through the crowd, out of the hold of the ship, to a higher plane. The very next scene has Edie Doyle (Eva Marie Saint) running along the rooftops, trying to find Terry to give him her murdered (we might be tempted to say "martyred") brother's coat to wear—to welcome him back into the fold of the righteous, if you will. In this shot, she is surrounded by nothing but the aerials on the rooftops, which look like a series of crucifixes. It is a landscape that seems to allow Kazan to stage, heavy-handedly, the message "I've been crucified" by doing the right thing. This is, at best, strange and problematic visual rhetoric.

SC
Episode 23 || 05/15/06

Noireme 072: *Kiss Me Deadly* (1955)

N = 00:56:17 ‖ RT = 01:46:02 ‖ RTP = 53.081%

LA ABSURD

While Mickey Spillane's 1952 novel *Kiss Me, Deadly* is set in New York City, the 1955 film *Kiss Me Deadly* is set in Los Angeles. The "character" of LA is an important player in the film. It's an absurd place to set a movie (in honesty, it's simply an absurd place), but the choice of moving this New York City hard-boiled novel to LA fits the other narrative changes the film makes. What was a story about political corruption, the Mafia, and narcotics becomes a story about our fears in a nuclear age—and fears of who knows what else—and given the absurdity of the film's story, it is wise to move the setting to LA. LA is a more frantic, simpler, and more outrageous city than New York, and this is a faster, simpler, more outrageous plot. It's glitzy and glamorous, and as over-the-top silly as LA itself.

SC

And the already hyperbolic city of Los Angeles is exaggerated in this film. We've seen many other films noir set in LA. But here, Los Angeles is photographed in an exaggerated fashion by director Robert Aldrich and cinematographer Ernest Laszlo. They focus on locations like the Angel's Flight funicular, a very important short rail line in the Bunker Hill region of Los Angeles. They give us exaggerated staircase shots, which we don't normally associate with Los Angeles. In essence, they give us a Los Angeles boiled down to Bunker Hill (at its urban center) and a beach house. And at that beach house, of course, they will stage one of the most extravagant and absurd endings to be found in any noir. All along the way, the filmmakers play with the actual Los Angeles as if it were a movie set—using wide-angle shots or extreme angle shots that distort, extend, or squeeze the spaces of Los Angeles like pieces of taffy.

RE
Episode 32 || 02/01/07

Noireme 073: *The Killers* (1946)

N = 00:54:33 ‖ RT = 01:52:04 ‖ RTP = 53.133%

In the absence of God, the meaning of existence is now founded on free will: that is the key theme in play in many films noir, especially *The Killers* (and in Camus's seminal existentialist treatise *The Myth of Sisyphus,* as discussed in noireme 034). For this reason, one of the most interesting characteristics of the femme fatale is that she confuses people into thinking they act of their free will, when in fact they act according to her will. In *The Killers,* Charleston (Vince Barnett) warns "The Swede" (Burt Lancaster) of this. Having seen "The Swede" spend hours with a memento given to him by Kitty (Ava Gardner)—a handkerchief with golden harps on it—and then seeing him out of sorts in Kitty's presence, Charleston warns him to "stop listening to those golden harps." But it's clear that's all "The Swede" thinks about; this token of Kitty's affection is speaking to him more clearly than reality.

SC
Episode 10 || 11/01/05

Noireme 074: *The Lady from Shanghai* (1947)

N = 00:46:36 || RT = 01:27:26 || RTP = 53.978%

Among the most calculating of all directors, Orson Welles is smart enough to realize when the script contains a really good line and to bring it back in words or images as a structuring motif. In *The Lady from Shanghai,* Mr. and Mrs. Bannister (Everett Sloane and Rita Hayworth) are always at each other's throats. During a long yacht trip with them, crewman Michael O'Hara (Welles) tires of their arguments and relates a story of when he was once fishing at night and saw the most incredible site: "an ocean of blood," where he caught a shark, the shark bled in the water, other sharks started feeding on it, and pretty soon they all destroyed each other. Initially, this anecdote is in the script, but then it is figured into the camera work as well. O'Hara later arranges to meet Mrs. Bannister clandestinely at the aquarium in San Francisco. She comes under the pretense of wanting to warn him that he is involving himself in an intrigue that is going to get him into a bind, and he comes thinking he is in control of the intrigue. As they have their conversation, sharks circle behind them in the background, in waters of the aquarium, suggesting these two may also be caught up in a sort of feeding frenzy.

SC
Episode 15 || 01/15/06

Noireme 075: *Laura* (1944)

N = 00:47:17 ‖ RT = 01:27:07 ‖ RTP = 54.276%

A motif that helps structure Otto Preminger's film *Laura* is David Raksin's famous score music entitled "Laura's Theme." "Laura's Theme" serves a lot of the same functions as the visual motifs in this film—the clock, the handheld baseball game, or the eponymous painting—for it reveals character traits. In ways that have been justly lauded in film history, this is an interesting use of score; frequently, it's not being used to create tension to underscore the action for the audience so much as to reveal the subjective states of mind of key characters.

RE

It's true that this theme is not a typical motif, for motifs rarely do so much to reveal the internal emotional states of characters. Then again, this film is full of such atypical and revelatory motifs. The dramatic entrances to scenes function similarly to the score, revealing a great deal about the internal life of the character.

SC

Moreover, Raksin makes a strong choice in playing the theme on different instruments; in certain scenes, the score progresses from a lush orchestral moment to single instruments, all the way down to being banged out with one finger on a piano. But some version of the theme underscores virtually every significant event in this film, as when detective Mark McPherson (Dana Andrews) is dreaming of Laura (Gene Tierney) right before her surprise reappearance; the theme is playing as Mark is suddenly awakened to this new reality.

RE
Episode 9 ‖ 10/14/05

Noireme 076: *The Killers* (1946)

N = 00:55:46 || RT = 01:52:04 || RTP = 54.318%

N = 01:07:50

In *The Killers,* at the very moment characters understand they have made a mistake—that is, they recognize their own agency in their demise—the killers appear as if out of nowhere, materializing like fate itself coming to take care of things. Ole Andersen, "The Swede" (Burt Lancaster), seems to be the only character in the film who never actually sees a reflection of himself, which raises the question of whether he ever gets a sense of the importance or implications of his own decisions and actions. There is a visual clue in the film that lets the viewer know at what point in the story each of these characters has gone astray and has made a fatally flawed decision: the character sees himself in a mirror. While at some point in the flashback narrations the other characters look in the mirror, "The Swede" never does. It's right after a character looks in the mirror that we are shown the moment in their story that is their undoing. A clear example is the deathbed confession of "Blinky" (Jeff Corey). As is true of all the individual, interlocking character narratives, Blinky's story is told in flashback, and it focuses on the moment when Big Jim (Albert Dekker) assembled the team to pull off the heist. And at the end of that scene, Blinky fixes his tie in the mirror before he leaves the room, and it's that moment when he sees himself and realizes he has just made a fateful decision, a decision that could go astray, and that lets the viewer know he knows he has done something wrong. There's a similar mirror scene for just about everyone in the story except Ole, making us wonder if director Robert Siodmak is suggesting that the real tragedy of Ole's character is that he never has the self-awareness that would allow him to take principled action—either to continue the fight or to commit suicide. Instead, he simply gives up; fate (that is, the killers) deals with him just as surely, but for different reasons.

SC
Episode 10 || 11/01/05

Noireme 077: *The Postman Always Rings Twice* (1946)

N = 01:05:03 ‖ RT = 01:52:50 ‖ RTP = 57.651%

N = 01:15:59

Certain in framings of Frank Chambers (John Garfield) in *The Postman Always Rings Twice* demonstrate the visual style of noir and its narrative efficacy. When Frank enters the diner, where most of the action will take place, for the first time, there's a complicated patch of light and shadow on the wall in the background, against which he's framed as he takes a stool at the counter. There is light angling in through the windows of the diner, obviously passing through a latticework outside and casting almost triangular geometric shadows on the wall. Thus, the first scene in which we see Frank, he is already framed within a netlike grid, trapped from the very get-go. An almost identical composition repeats later on in the film, right after Frank and Cora (Lana Turner) plan and execute the "accidental" death of Cora's husband Nick (Cecil Kellaway). Frank wakes up in the hospital. The district attorney (Leon Ames) comes in, and he's trying to frame Frank. We see Frank framed against the same slant of light and geometric shadows. But this time the crisscrossed shadows look more like bars, and we get the sense he's truly trapped. In the earlier occurrences of this composition, the light and shadow slope from high left to low right; in other words, the pattern seems to be moving in the direction one moves when reading, forward in space and time. Significantly, in the latter occurrences of this composition, the angle is reversed. We see this framing again at the moment Frank has a falling out with Cora. He has been convinced by his lawyer Arthur Keats (Hume Cronyn) to sign a statement ratting her out. They're brought into a private room where Keats has told Cora that she can make a confession if she so chooses. She's making that confession, looking down at Frank, and there's a clear sight line from her eyes to his, matched by a shadow cast on the wall right behind their heads. This shadow is part of the same composition we've seen, but it is cast at the reverse angle from the first two scenes in which it occurred, this time demonstrating not only that Frank is trapped in this fabrication but also that his story is running in reverse, that his future is all behind him.

SC

Episode 30 || 12/01/06

Noireme 078: *Laura* (1944)

N = 00:53:43 ‖ RT = 01:27:07 ‖ RTP = 61.660%

There are few moments in the film *Laura* that look particularly noir, which is surprising in light of the fact this is often considered one the great, and prototypal, films noir. It certainly manages to create a noir atmosphere, but it does so largely in the absence of a noir visual style, which makes it an interesting film to study. Gone are the high-contrast, low-key lighting schemes, the heavy foreground obstructions. Instead, this film looks back in time to classic studio-era interiors such as were created for big budget MGM films—elegant spaces, flooded in light. Here, noir is not a dark and foreboding cityscape; it is a place of elegant interiors. But there are at least four key moments when a noir vision bubbles up to the surface and artfully blemishes that smooth, well-lit facade. The first of those—striking when it happens because it stands in contrast to what has preceded—is at the moment when Laura (Gene Tierney) returns to her apartment and Detective McPherson (Dana Andrews) calls down to the basement where he has another cop bugging her phone. The scene cuts to the basement, where we see the cop with his jacket off, feet up on the table, and hat at a rakish angle. There's a single lamp hanging above, shining down a harsh light that illuminates this rough cop and a few details of a dark, dank basement. This is a beautifully composed noir scene, and its look anticipates many noir framings of cop work—tough, dirty cop work in police procedurals of 1946 and 1947, and darker still in many private detective pictures later on.

SC
Episode 9 || 10/14/05

Noireme 079: *The Big Lebowski* (1998)

N = 01:18:03 ‖ RT = 01:57:16 ‖ RTP = 66.558%

DEFECTIVE DETECTIVE WORK

In their noir-inflected film *The Big Lebowski,* one of the ways the Coen brothers rework the conventions of the hard-boiled detective genre is through the use of parody. The Dude (Jeff Bridges) is called to the house of porn magnate Jackie Treehorn (Ben Gazzara), for whom The Dude has been causing some trouble while conducting his amateur "investigation." Treehorn interrupts their conversation, to take what he pretends to be an important phone call, and jots down a number on a pad of paper. The Dude, having seen films noir, goes up to the pad with a pencil and traces in graphite what Treehorn wrote. The Coen brothers have a lot of fun with The Dude's (and by extension, the audience's) expectations in this moment, for it turns out what Treehorn scribbled was a meaningless pornographic doodle. In this updating of noir, the moment the amateur sleuth actually tries to apply real sleuthing techniques, the results are defective—revealing nothing for The Dude, but a great deal for the audience about how the Coens enjoy playing with noir conventions.

RE
Episode 11 || 11/15/05

Noireme 080: *Laura* (1944)

N = 00:59:11 ‖ RT = 01:27:07 ‖ RTP = 67.936%

N = 01:11:56

In noireme 078 ("Undercover"), we noted there are only four or five key moments when a noir vision bubbles up to the surface and artfully blemishes *Laura*'s smooth, well-lit facade. In addition to the scene in the basement, there are two other moments later in the film with a recognizably noir visual style. Detective Mark McPherson (Dana Andrews) confronts Shelby (Vincent Price) about what happened to Laura and whether Shelby tried to kill her. The scene is framed with Shelby in the foreground, so much so that he obstructs a large part of the frame and is nearly out of focus, and McPherson in the background, facing the camera with a shadow over his eyes as he's interviewing Shelby. This composition conveys McPherson's intensity and suggests his forthrightness and fitness for the job, while implying Price's uncertain and shadowy motives. Later, when McPherson takes Laura herself (Gene Tierney) to the station to interrogate her, the visual style again becomes recognizably noir. What immediately precedes this scene is a nod back to the parlor mysteries of the thirties, when everyone is brought together, all the suspects in one room, and the detective says something to the effect of "I'm about to bring the killer in." The scene sets up an expectation of quick resolution, à la *The Thin Man,* but instead something strange happens. Mark hauls Laura into the station and throws her under the harsh interrogation lamps, not to unveil her culpability, but rather to find out if she cares about him. At the moment we think we're seeing noir in the service of intrigue and plot resolution, we get noir in the service of a love story. It's a strange twist, and another reason it is problematic to consider *Laura* a prototypal noir.

SC
Episode 9 || 10/14/05

Noireme 081: *The Big Lebowski* (1998)

N = 01:20:11 ‖ RT = 01:57:16 ‖ RTP = 68.377%

N = 01:22:21

The Big Lebowski contains a bizarre and elaborate dream sequence that, despite appearances, has its roots in the hard-boiled detective genre and in the film noir style. Ethan Coen highlighted these sources in an interview: "Another convention of PI Movies, I mean Raymond Chandler's stories, is at some point the PI gets slugged, or gets slipped a Mickey Finn, goes into some sort of delirium or hallucination of the movies and the many novels the movies are based on. We have license to do it by virtue of the genre."

SC

When The Dude (Jeff Bridges) is slipped a Mickey (i.e., a hallucinogenic) by porn magnate Jackie Treehorn (Ben Gazzara), the "Gutterballs" dream sequence erupts. It's so elaborate and so defining a scene that some fans want to go so far as to claim *The Big Lebowski* is a sub-genre unto itself: bowling noir. But the sequence also reveals more information about the character of The Dude, a pothead and an avid bowler. Propelled by the song "I Just Checked In to See What Condition My Condition Was In," by Kenny Rogers and The First Edition, this memorable dream sequence brings together references to bowling, film trailers, Busby Berkeley musicals, Saddam Hussein, and Wagnerian Opera. "Gutterballs" functions as a movie within a movie, even opening with its own credits kicked off with "Jackie Treehorn Presents." While the sequence is inspired by hard-boiled fiction and film noir, the result is a pop-culture mashup that delightfully showcases the Coen brothers' humor and self-consciousness as they play with and against well-known noir conventions.

RE
Episode 11 || 11/15/05

Noireme 082: *It's a Wonderful Life* (1946)

N = 01:29:27 ‖ RT = 02:10:24 ‖ RTP = 68.597%

N = 01:30:25

There are many episodes in *It's a Wonderful Life* that are exceedingly noir in both theme and style, and one of the most poignant is the moment when George Bailey (James Stewart) stands before his family and destroys the symbols of his youthful dreams. In a long sequence, over six minutes, he's brutal to his wife and children; he's so disillusioned he has nothing left to give, and he turns on them. The sequence ends when he kicks apart the model buildings and bridges he has spent his lifetime building—always having dreamed of being an engineer, of escaping his tiny hometown and building something great for humankind. Now he destroys those dreams, and they lie dashed. He turns to his wife Mary (Donna Reed), who asks, "Why are you torturing the children like this?" He says her name once, almost like a plea, like there's a question in his voice. He turns and passes by the camera on his way out and goes partially out of frame and entirely out of focus as his left ear passes very close to the camera (the ear that went deaf when he saved his young brother in childhood). In this almost five-second sequence as he's leaving, it goes entirely silent. It's almost as if the camera and the silence move us inside the head of man who has lost his focus, who has lost control.

SC
Episode 13 || 12/15/05

Noireme 083: *Gun Crazy* (1950)

N = 01:03:03 ‖ RT = 01:27:01 ‖ RTP = 72.457%

N = 01:18:49

As discussed in noireme 008 ("Into the Countryside"), *Out of the Past* opens with an atypical noir shot, of a big, dark-suited driver and his hat, looking out over the dashboard as he drives into a small, sun-bathed, rural town. Instead of noir telling its usual tales of urban corruption, this shot suggests that crime is so pervasive that it has gone everywhere; it has found the small town. *Gun Crazy* also explores what happens when the city loses its grip on noir narratives but gives a different spin on these themes. Unlike Jeff Bailey (Robert Mitchum) in *Out of the Past,* what Bart Tare (John Dall) and Annie Starr (Peggy Cummins) are trying to find throughout *Gun Crazy* is not an innocent place (and thus a place of refuge) so much as a place to stake out and call their own. The film ends with them fleeing into the countryside, and this forced flight washes all the glimmer and glitz off of their dreams. No sooner are they cornered than they drive off into the countryside, bust through a gate, and fall down into the muck. Just moments before, we saw them dressed up in furs, dancing the night away in an elegant club. How quickly it can all change.

SC

In addition to playing with the city/country distinction, this film deploys another pervasive motif of the postwar period, the carnival. Shown to be a space of societal dissolution, the carnival is a place where we (already) know everyone is going to get ripped off, where all types of games are really just a version of the grift, but we still desperately search for enjoyment. Director Joseph Lewis and the screenwriters (one of whom is Dalton Trumbo, though he is uncredited because he was already blacklisted) suggest that between the city and the countryside was a temporary zone of mobility—the traveling carnival. The boundaries between the country and the city, and between what was pure and what was corrupt, appear more permeable in this picture. Through the mediating site of the carnival, the corruption of the city is transported and transplanted into the countryside, and the country becomes a site of disillusionment and trauma.

RE

Episode 17 || 02/15/06

Noireme 084: *The Lady from Shanghai* (1947)

N = 01:03:26 ‖ RT = 01:27:26 ‖ RTP = 72.551%

ON TRIAL

Orson Welles's *The Lady from Shanghai* is a film characterized by constant and restless action, in terms of the diegesis and the mise-en-scène. Welles pulls out all the stops in the trial sequence, including an unusually active jury box, and an attorney, Arthur Bannister (Everett Sloane), who cross-exams himself. The accompanying, very unusual, camera angles in this sequence are motivated to further underscore this action. There is a point-of-view shot from the witness stand to the jury box as the jurors explode into laughter at Bannister's antics, and another from Michael O'Hara's (Orson Welles) point of view, looking at people on the witness stand. Even the latter, which by all accounts should be a relatively static view, captures numerous little bits of action. At one point, a key dialogue is interrupted because a juror gets a cough; at another, a juror makes a joke. This trial sequence is evidence of Welles's overall approach to *The Lady from Shanghai:* even outside of such famous scenes as the funhouse mirror sequence, the backdrops to the diegetic action of this film are teeming with life and animated characters—from the jury box to the San Francisco aquarium, from Acapulco to Chinatown. This is a film where the background itself seems to be shifting and moving. This is a world teeming with life, while it's on the precipice of death.

RE
Episode 15 || 01/15/06

Noireme 085: *Kiss Me Deadly* (1955)

N = 01:25:15 ‖ RT = 01:46:02 ‖ RTP = 80.399%

N = 01:26:30

Mickey Spillane's novel *Kiss Me, Deadly* portrays a monstrously criminal postwar America, sick with greed to the very highest levels of society. Spillane's antidote to this sickness is Mike Hammer, a lone wolf who fears nothing but fear itself, who ruthlessly hunts down the monster in order to protect him and his. Though Spillane might have felt otherwise, I would maintain that such a man can't be the solution when he possesses all of the characteristics of the problem. We don't need a vaccine; we need a cure for a full-blown disease. But in the marrow of Hammer's bones, there is a conviction that things must change, and in his blood flows the anger of righteous indignation. Hammer thinks with his muscles, and Ralph Meeker is a properly self-absorbed actor who has the right wolfish grin and biceps, and ultimately those are the only characteristics Hammer need possess. Screenwriter Albert Isaac Bezzerides finds the perfect turn of phrase for framing this new noir hero, adding an early line in the film that does not exist in the book. Christina Bailey (Cloris Leachmen) says to Hammer, "You only have one real lasting love. You." Indeed, Hammer's honor is self-serving: his only mission is to take revenge on any who have wronged him or those he holds dear. He is a hunter who revels in the thrill of killing men who pose a threat and possessing women who seem "hungry." And all men seem to pose a threat, and all women seem to hunger for Mike Hammer. For these reasons, I would suggest he is the sort of protagonist who put an end to hard-boiled fiction as it had been before Spillane and an end to film noir as it had been before *Kiss Me Deadly*. What he killed was nuance—noir's tendency to deal with the finer shades of gray.

SC

Mike Hammer is the übermale who completely breaks other men down into pansies. All it really takes for him to get the information he needs are two good, swift backhands across the jaw.

RE
Episode 32 || 02/01/07

Noireme 086: *Batman Begins* (2005)

N = 01:55:23 ‖ RT = 02:19:52 ‖ RTP = 82.495%

N = 01:52:29

Christopher Nolan's Batman in *Batman Begins* is truly a dark knight—a noir protagonist, driven by guilt, fear, uncertainty, and a past that continues to haunt him and that he can't let go of. Nolan tries to reimagine Batman as a vigilante hero, as a way of restoring order in a post–September 11, 2001, culture of fear, and he draws pointed analogies with the current U.S. political climate in 2005; his superhero-noir story becomes an allegory that critiques the ongoing Global War on Terror. After September 11, a person who dresses up in a bat costume and tries to exorcise the demons of a city will not only confront the isolated case of supervillainy but also the harder problem of a society living in that culture of fear. The motif of the smoke that envelopes Gotham City—the visible release of a fear-inducing gas, whose sole purpose is to create terror—suggests an all-encompassing, all-consuming wave of fear that not even a superhero can dispel.

RE

In terms of the culture of fear post 9/11, *Batman Begins* is a fascinating meditation because ultimately the weapon of mass destruction is fear itself. The film manages to convey the fact that no other weapon need be found; if you simply instill fear in a populace, it will destroy itself.

SC
Episode 3 || 07/15/05

Noireme 087: *Touch of Evil* (1958)

N = 01:34:21 || RT = 01:50:41 || RTP = 85.243%

Toward the end of *Touch of Evil,* a drunken and despondent Captain Hank Quinlan (Orson Welles) finds the strength to stand up and go out to talk to his accuser, Sergeant Pete Menzies (Joseph Calleia). Menzies is trying to lure him out of Tanya's (Marlene Dietrich) house, away from the pianola music that is playing a nostalgic old-world tune that is soothing Quinlan. There is an incredible shot as Quinlan rises up, and on the wall behind him is a bull's head with the spears from the bullfight sticking from it. The shot is held for a few seconds, creating in the eye of the beholder an equivalency between Quinlan and the mounted bull's head on the wall. And it is important to note that Quinlan is not associated with just any slaughtered bull: this was a prized bull, taken down by a matador in front of a stadium of spectators. It is hard not to see this as Orson Welles's commentary on his own cinematic death. He is going to die like the prized bull in the ring; it is not just a shallow, meaningless death but one he is going to play up for all of its spectacular power. Welles came into fame in his early twenties and by twenty-five had worked as a theater producer on Broadway; the *War of the Worlds* radio broadcaster; the voice of the Shadow; and the director *Citizen Kane.* With a shot such as this, Welles seems to intuit that *Touch of Evil* might be his exit from mainstream filmmaking, and his departure is going to be nothing less than spectacular.

RE

Episode 31 || 01/01/07

Noireme 088: *It's a Wonderful Life* (1946)

N = 01:52:51 ‖ RT = 02:10:24 ‖ RTP = 86.541%

N = 01:53:30

In *It's a Wonderful Life,* George Bailey (James Stewart) feels his life has amounted to nothing and contemplates suicide. To dissuade him, George's guardian angel gives him the chance to see what would have been had he never lived. In the absence of George Bailey—and his father, and the Bailey Bros. Building and Loan Association—Bedford Falls has become a noir town. The suggestion is that, if it weren't for small town heroes, the very sorts of despicable and disreputable things—noir things—that draw people to big cities would be drawn to small towns. Now the town is called Pottersville, after the film's antagonist, the greedy and domineering banker Mr. Potter (Lionel Barrymore). What was a nice little white sign that said "You Are Now in Bedford Falls" is replaced by a flashing neon sign that says "Pottersville." There is nothing left but pool halls, pawn shops, and dance halls, and what was the town theater is now a strip club. As George comes running up to the spot that used to be the Building and Loan, he looks in agony at that space that was once his family's business. In the background behind him there is a dance hall, and the upstairs windows have white shades that are drawn, capturing silhouettes projected forward from inside — couples dancing closely and seductively, as shadows against those shades. At that very moment, as George is standing and staring at the club that has taken the place of the Building and Loan, we see the name of the club is Dreamland, and we recognize how dark the noir dream is, and how pervasive. Noir has begun to influence all genres of American filmmaking, even the holiday family drama.

SC
Episode 13 || 12/15/05

Noireme 089: *He Walked by Night* (1948)

N = 01:10:14 ‖ RT = 01:19:03 ‖ RTP = 88.847%

Cinematographer John Alton is a master of visual storytelling, and his style is memorable in its interplay of formal composition and narrative function. Consider the tense moments before the criminal Roy Morgan (Richard Basehart) is cornered by the police in *He Walked by Night*. Tension is built without dialogue through visual design and sound effects. The play of light and shadow, and the incredible use of low-key lighting, fully ensnarl Roy Morgan in an ever-tightening mise-en-scène that becomes more and more prisonlike. In a film like *He Walked by Night,* Alton perhaps exercises his talents more fully than if he had been a cinematographer at MGM or Twentieth Century Fox. Working within the financial constraints of this low-budget Eagle-Lion film, Alton delivered a visual style that was not expensive but rather visually expansive.

RE
Episode 25 || 06/14/06

Noireme 090: *The Killing* (1956)

N = 01:17:34 ‖ RT = 01:25:09 ‖ RTP = 91.094%

N = 01:17:40

In *The Killing,* repeated sounds—most often the sound of the starting bell of the horse race at the center of the intrigue—help the viewer make sense of the nonlinear narrative. But there are also *visual* repetitions within the husband and wife subplot that similarly punctuate and structure the story. The fact that George Peatty (Elisha Cook Jr.) is, from the beginning, shown through bars lets us know to what extent he is always trapped by his domestic reality. The first time we see George he is at the racetrack, for he's the betting clerk. We see him framed through the bars at the betting window, but we can't initially tell by the angle and distance from which the shot is taken whether he is at the betting window or is in prison. Later, as the heist is being carried out, George comes up to a staircase and holds on to the balusters. Again, it looks like he is behind bars, with the dark space behind him looming like the reality of prison life (and his domestic life). Finally, there is a scene that sums up the whole domestic subplot (and to some extent we could argue it is not a subplot but rather the heart of the plot itself, for in noir it is very often the moment when emotion or passion trumps cool thinking that everything comes unraveled, and that's the case with the George and Sherry subplot). George comes home unexpectedly and finds his wife Sherry (Marie Windsor) waiting not for him but rather for her lover whom she has sent to knock off George. George enters, and he is framed standing next to the birdcage. He and Sherry have an argument, and even now she is cold-hearted—completely indifferent as he stands there bleeding out from the injuries he sustained at the hands of her hired killer. In essence, her message to George in this moment amounts to "You need to get out of here; you're spoiling things." George reaches a point of no return and shoots her. She falls; then he collapses to the ground and the birdcage goes over with him. There is a telling shot that pans from his bloody face to the birdcage right next to him as the bird says "not fair, not fair," repeating what were Sherry's last words. Here, at the crux of the narrative, repeated sonic and visual motifs unite to structure a nonlinear story that might otherwise be hard to follow and to layer that story with additional resonances.

SC

Episode 19 || 03/15/06

Noireme 091: *He Walked by Night* (1948)

N = 01:13:16 ‖ RT = 01:19:03 ‖ RTP = 92.684%

N = 01:15:19

There are several cinematic touches in *He Walked by Night* that are important to film history, for example, the numerous sewer scenes in this movie that are beautifully filmed, illuminated only by the characters running through the sewers holding flashlights. All we see are the characters receding into an increasingly small form of light, with darkness all around. In the case of the criminal Roy Morgan (Richard Basehart) running through the sewer, we see his light bobbing erratically and illuminating his way poorly as he sprints alone through a narrow sewer. This is juxtaposed with the slowly advancing, brighter light of the unified police force as they advance down a broad, square sewer line. This simple but carefully calculated lighting and mise-en-scène give us the sense that the outcome is inevitable, that the combined force of the law is too much and Roy will never escape. It is important to note that this film came out one year before *The Third Man*. While the sewer scenes in the latter are often discussed as cinematic innovations, few have noted they are almost identical to the shots by cinematographer John Alton and directors Alfred L. Werker and Anthony Mann in *He Walked by Night;* while their very composition is enough to suggest *The Third Man* director Carol Reed's debt, it is also worth noting that *He Walked by Night* was a product of Eagle-Lion pictures, a British production company established to release British pictures in the United States and to create American B pictures to share the billing in Britain with British releases, thus greatly increasing the likelihood that Reed was familiar with *He Walked by Night* when he filmed *The Third Man*.

SC
Episode 25 || 06/14/06

Noireme 092: *Touch of Evil* (1958)

N = 01:42:59 ‖ RT = 01:50:41 ‖ RTP = 93.043%

N = 01:42:58

Touch of Evil can be seen as a meditation on filmmaking. The final sequence of "Mike" Vargas (Charlton Heston) trying to record the conversation between Sergeant Pete Menzies (Joseph Calleia) and corrupt Captain Hank Quinlan (Orson Welles), going through the muck and the oil rigs with a recording device, is a metaphor for filmmaking itself. On the set, these actors are being followed by filmmaking crews, and when Welles as Quinlan is standing on the bridge, and he hears the echo of the recording device, Welles the director is making a self-conscious pun on filmmaking. Welles knows the scene is actually double microphoned, because he is also recording the scene for us in the audience. In the action and the mise-en-scène, he is exploiting these doublings and double entendres on every level in the final scenes of this film.

RE

Ultimately, the question is what options remain when a film becomes this self-reflexive? The self-conscious auteur of such a work has to write himself out of the picture in the end, for there is nowhere else to go. The perfect moment of filmic punning, this double gesture, both narrative and extra-narrative, is illustrated in the death of Quinlan. As Vargas follows them around with a device to record their conversation, he gets closer and closer, until Quinlan hears a slightly delayed echo of his own voice from the device. In other words, the film stages the closing of the gap until there is just the slightest delay, the slightest separation in space and time, between Welles the director and Welles the actor, between the extranarrative stuff of filmmaking and the narrative that is being constructed. At the moment these join, the auteur must die, and right after he hears the slight echo of his own voice, Quinlan is killed.

SC

Episode 31 || 01/01/07

Noireme 093: *The Set-Up* (1949)

N = 01:07:31 ‖ RT = 01:12:27 ‖ RTP = 93.191%

The sounds of *The Set-Up* are diegetically motivated: even the music in the film comes from identifiable sources within the story world and can be heard by both the audience and the characters in the action. Moreover, this film uses no prerecorded orchestral music playing in the background; there is no underscore to manipulate our emotions. *The Set-Up* cannot build up the emotional impact of the boxing matches the way director Sylvester Stallone did in *Rocky,* by cranking up swelling underscore music that gets our heart pumping. Instead, the excitement in the ring comes from the sound of the punches, from the bell that's rung, from the sounds of the audience. Then, as if to underscore the brutality of Stoker Thompson's (Robert Ryan) world, there is a jazz riff to accompany his beating at the hands of mob thugs after the fight, and again the jazz band is part of this world—the bandmates represented by shadows on the wall of an alley, the very dead-end alley where Stoker's beating is meted out.

RE
Episode 18 || 03/01/06

Noireme 094: *Chinatown* (1974)

N = 02:02:35 ‖ RT = 02:10:25 ‖ RTP = 93.994%

In *Chinatown,* we get a cultural history of Los Angeles that, in the hands of a lesser filmmaker than Polanski, could make for horrible storytelling: how does this film make a water-and-power subplot—about the development of the valley communities of Los Angeles—interesting? Because, like *The Maltese Falcon,* the water-and-power story is ultimately about "the stuff that dreams are made of." When Jake Gittes (Jack Nicholson) finally confronts Noah Cross, played by the inimitable actor John Huston (who also directed *The Maltese Falcon*), he asks, "Why are you doing this?" Why, in essence, are you diverting this water when you already have more money than you will ever need? Why, Gittes seems to be asking, are you pursuing an equivalent of the Maltese Falcon? Cross's response to Gittes is "The Future, Mr. Gitts. The future." In *Chinatown,* there is a phantasm that everyone's willing to die or kill for, that leads to deceit and betrayal as inevitably as it does in *The Maltese Falcon.* However, Robert Towne's script—as opposed to the ending of *The Maltese Falcon* where Sydney Greenstreet and Peter Lorre set off on one more treasure hunt—suggests that Noah Cross will see real, tangible benefits of his actions in his future. So, at the same time that we have a protagonist, Jake Gittes, who seems almost perversely incapable of untangling this giant mystery, we also have possibly the most real and largest political corruption story in any film noir. This film can be read as an allegory of the founding of Southern California and, by extension, probably of the Hollywood dream factories themselves. And it is significant that this dialogue is spoken by John Huston, a noir filmmaker in his own right and whose on-screen presence brings together noir's past and its future.

RE
Episode 24 || 05/31/06

Noireme 095: *The Grifters* (1990)

N = 01:46:05 ‖ RT = 01:50:19 ‖ RTP = 96.163%

Perhaps the best noir dialogue in *The Grifters* occurs late in the film, at the moment when Lilly Dillon (Angelica Huston) tries to convince her son Roy Dillon (John Cusack) that he's got to get out of the racket. She says, "Grift is like anything else. You don't stand still. You either go up, or you go down. Usually down, sooner or later." And that analogy is so powerful that it later impacts the way director Stephen Frears frames the story. From this moment on, the film looks increasingly noir, and it picks up on the motif of the elevator—so prominent in films noir since *The Maltese Falcon*—to show what the fate of these characters is, and what their relative positions are, in the film. At the end, we get one of the most magnificent noir shots since the classical noir period, of Angelica Huston after she's committed the final and most vicious of all crimes. It's a shot of the elevator going down, repeated several times as if we're seeing her descent from each floor. And every floor is entirely dark, only the elevator illuminated, focusing our attention on the magnitude and irreversibility of her crime and punishment as she descends, and descends.

SC
Episode 16 || 02/01/06

Noireme 096: *The Killing* (1956)

N = 01:22:11 || RT = 01:25:09 || RTP = 96.516%

The final sequences of *The Killing* masterfully demonstrate the role of fate in the noir universe. Toward the end of the film, even as the other members of the heist crew meet their demise, Johnny Clay (Sterling Hayden) still can make his getaway and abscond with the stolen money from the racetrack. Clay goes into a secondhand store to buy a suitcase in order to hide the money. But because he's improvising and needs to get out of town fast, he ends up buying a suitcase with busted locks. That's a flaw in the plan—a bit of random chance—that will eventually sabotage Johnny Clay's escape plan, and director Stanley Kubrick suspensefully piles on coincidence after coincidence until the weight of all the random chance is too much. Clay can't carry the bag onto the airplane because it is too large to fit into the overhead bin, and he has to check the bag instead. Then what happens? There's a tiny little poodle that gets away from its owner and runs onto the tarmac in front of the baggage cart. In order to avoid hitting the poodle, the baggage handler has to swerve. Clay's suitcase falls off the cart and hits the runway. Due to the broken lock, it springs open and all of the money spills out. Clay then sees the stolen cash in a swirling vortex on the tarmac—forever beyond his reach. But even that moment doesn't seal Clay's fate, for he can still try to escape. But as he leaves the terminal, his only chance to get away is in a cab. He spots one, but it pulls away from the curb seconds too soon. But even then he could still run away on foot, as his girlfriend Fay (Coleen Gray) urges him to do. However, at this point Clay gives up and deadpans, "Ah, what's the difference?" Never has there been a better depiction of how, in the noir universe, all wrongdoing is ultimately punished; fate always evens the score.

RE
Episode 19 || 03/15/06

Noireme 097: *Kiss Me Deadly* (1955)

N = 01:43:16 || RT = 01:46:02 || RTP = 97.391%

In noiremes 005 ("The Erotic and the Neurotic") and 072 ("LA Absurd"), we have suggested the 1955 film *Kiss Me Deadly* conflates the erotic and the neurotic, and that conflation goes well with the changes made to the plot of the novel when it was adapted to film. The film is no longer about political corruption and narcotics; it's about something very different. Ultimately, it's about the irresistible appeal of danger in the nuclear era, and thus the thing in the box at the end is not narcotics but rather the unleashed force from some sort of Pandora's box. In this sense, the final shots of this film announce the final shots of *Raiders of the Lost Ark,* the opening of the covenant. And in that later film by Steven Spielberg, the people who manage to avert their eyes and not give in to looking at whatever is in the box are the ones who survive. We get the same themes here, which makes us wonder if the women in this film are both erotic and neurotic because they're supposed to remind us that to look too much is ultimately our undoing.

SC
Episode 32 || 02/01/07

Noireme 098: *Sunset Blvd.* (1950)

N = 01:48:04 ‖ RT = 01:50:12 ‖ RTP = 98.064%

In "Some Visual Motifs of Film Noir," Janey Place and Lowell Peterson discuss several motifs that establish the world of noir. To their list I would add another—the visual trope of the staircase. It's surprising how many films noir prominently feature a staircase and how often that staircase serves as a representation of reversals of fate (think *Double Indemnity, The Killers, The Asphalt Jungle, Notorious,* etc.). *Sunset Blvd.* may have the greatest use of this trope; truly, the film hangs in the balance between an ascent and a descent. When Joe Gillis (William Holden) first enters Norma Desmond's (Gloria Swanson) house, he is mistaken for the undertaker, there to bring the coffin for Desmond's pet monkey. (The line between tragedy and comedy in this film is very thin.) He is admitted by the butler, Max (Erich von Stroheim), who is also Norma's first husband and the director who first discovered her (here, too, we have a reversal of fate, for the man who had been in charge has become the servant), and immediately Max leads Joe up the huge, spiraling staircase. It gives us false hope that maybe this case of mistaken identity is going to work to his advantage. But as he gets to the top of that staircase, Max says to him, "If you need help with the coffin, call me." This initial, ironic, inverted use of the motif is balanced against another at the very end of the film, when we are presented with Desmond's famous descent. She has killed Gillis, and while the newsmen have assembled to shoot footage of the killer, she believes they're there to capture her next great scene—one that will affirm her reascent into the firmament of great stars. As she comes down the staircase Max is once again in the role of "director," pretending to call the shots for the news crews rather than shatter her all-encompassing fantasy. The sheer madness of it all is captured in slow motion, as if her vision of things could freeze the world, fix it. As she comes down to the cameras we realize this spiraling descent, that she thinks is her ascent toward stardom, is her descent into madness. It is this misreading on her part that is the central tragedy of the film, and director Billy Wilder's greatest filmic irony in a film built upon such bitter ironies.

SC

Episode 21 || 04/15/06

Noireme 099: *The Maltese Falcon* (1941)

N = 00:06:58 || RT = 01:40:29 || RTP = 06.933%

One idea that comes full circle in *The Maltese Falcon* is that the characters in this film are desperately living in a present that offers no future, and yet have no past they can retreat into. Film noir dances between past, present, and future, and all three of these frames—in fact, time itself—represent a damaged concept. And into that breach, *The Maltese Falcon* gives an object, the falcon itself—this jewel-encrusted bird, this thing of legends, this artifact given to Charles V of Spain—that anchors all these characters' pursuits. It is an object from out of the past for which these characters are willing to give up their presents and risk their futures. As a narrative device, it is one of the greatest Hitchcockian MacGuffins in movie history—an object at the center of the plot that the characters are chasing but ultimately an object that is not important in itself. It is just some *thing*. But because the characters buy into it, it controls all their actions and relationships. Here, on one level, is a shameless plot device that becomes, within the American cultural consciousness, the stuff that dreams are made of.

RE
Episode 5 || 08/15/05

Noireme 100: *The Asphalt Jungle* (1950)

N = 01:50:42 ‖ RT = 01:52:04 ‖ RTP = 98.780%

The Asphalt Jungle seems to portray the displacement of America's rural population, its move to the city, as a sign of the erosion of the American Dream. In the early forties, the city could still be portrayed as a place of glamour and opportunity. But in *The Asphalt Jungle,* we see it as a place where the downtrodden go once they lose their possibility for a piece of the American landscape. So many of the characters in *The Asphalt Jungle* aren't moving forward because they're always thinking back in time. All Dix Handley wants is to recover the farm that he lost. We get the sense that everyone in this film is longing for a simpler past, a rural idyllic time that may or may not ever have existed. And we wonder if this isn't true of America as a whole. When we look at the city that John Huston portrays here—grimy, dangerous, and dilapidated—we can't help but feel a nostalgia for a prewar past, the sort of past people had (in movies, at least) before noir came along.

SC
Episode 8 || 10/01/05

Noireme 101: *The Big Sleep* (1946)

N = 01:53:43 ‖ RT = 01:53:51 ‖ RTP = 99.882%

CLEAN ENDINGS

At the end of *The Big Sleep*, all of the various loose threads of the mystery are pretty much known to the audience. The very last moments of the story return to the romance between Vivian Rutledge (Lauren Bacall) and Philip Marlowe (Humphrey Bogart). Marlowe grabs Rutledge by the arm and pulls her close. As a police siren approaches the house, the film ends with a series of glances between Marlowe and Rutledge. While looking into each other's eyes, first Marlowe, and then Rutledge, look offscreen toward the sound of the approaching siren before returning to a final shot of them gazing into each other's eyes. Marlowe and Rutledge are clearly going to stay together, though the siren and offscreen glances complicate a simplistic reading of this love match.

RE

And yet order is established, and it seems they may be redeemed by their love. They have been down and out, blackmailed, beat up, and kicked around—yet, at the end, order is established. Eddie Mars is gunned down, they care for one another, the police are coming, the sirens are there, and everything seems alright. Or does it? The film fades out to an image of two cigarettes smoldering together in a perfectly transparent ashtray. But as you suggest, this is noir; as cleanly as this film wants to tie things up, there is an opaque darkness lurking behind this suggestion of transparency and simple passion, this clean ending that may just go up in smoke.

SC
Episode 11 || 11/15/05

Noireme 102: *Gun Crazy* (1950)

N = 01:26:54 ‖ RT = 01:27:01 ‖ RTP = 99.885%

For much of the running time of *Gun Crazy,* Bart Tare (John Dall) and Annie Starr's (Peggy Cummins) crime spree seems to give their lives meaning. But nothing good lasts forever. Eventually, they're cornered by the hounds and the search team in a swamp. They're in the reeds at night, and they wake up in the morning to this fog-shrouded world where nothing is clear but they themselves and these dark reeds—then uncertainty all around. We hear voices, but they're disembodied. First, we hear the voice of Justice, the voice of Bart's buddy the sheriff, saying, "Bart . . . we're coming in to get you." Bart finally gets a chance to take a shot that matters, and in order to save his buddies he has to kill the woman he loves. But what impact does that have? It forces those he saved to respond to the gunfire. More, importantly, it further untethers the meaning of this whole tale. And so the film ends with a crane shot from above, of this little patch of reeds and these two dead bodies; as it pulls up into the sky, we see a little island in the midst of this fog-shrouded world. We're left to wonder, what matters now? What actions count? What is the epistemology of this world? What's grounding it? Where are we? And the fact of the matter is, we don't know anymore. In this postwar world, it's no longer clear.

SC
Episode 17 || 02/15/06

How We Wrote Our Noiremes

La lecture potentielle a le charme de faire ressortir la duplicité des textes, qu'ils soient
oulipiens ou non. (*Potential reading* has the charm of making manifest the duplicity of
texts, be they oulipian or not.) (Translation ours)
—Harry Mathews, "L'algorithme de Mathews"

"What is the use of a book," thought Alice, "without pictures or conversations?"
—Lewis Carroll, *Alice in Wonderland*[1]

THE TITLE OF THIS afterword is reminiscent of Italo Calvino's essay, "How I Wrote
One of My Books," in which he revealed the constraint under which he wrote *If on a
Winter's Night a Traveler*. It is common in oulipian work to reveal the constraint only at
the end. *A Void* ends with a wonderful "Post-scriptum" where Georges Perec reveals, in
the same lipogrammatic form as his entire novel, how and why he came to write a novel
without the letter *e*. And in the epigraph to the novel *The Name of the Rose*, Umberto
Eco acknowledges his debts to oulipian constraint, saying, "It is necessary to create constraints, to invent freely."

There are excellent reasons for not revealing at the outset that a text is written under
constraint, as doing so tends to overly focus the reader's attention on the constraint itself.
This too often results in the reader dismissing the constrained work as a gimmick and fail-
ing to notice or acknowledge the rich narrative and critical potentials of constraint. One
need not understand the constraint to appreciate Shakespeare's sonnets, Bach's fugues,
or Calvino's novels.

It struck us early in the preparation of this book that, if we were to write on constraint
and potential, we would need to practice what we preached. We would need to demonstrate constraint and potential in our very methodology. Therefore, not only are the
above noiremes themselves mathematically constrained (which we copped to early in this
investigation), but there is also a yet more profound constraint governing our text.

We used the "limited resource" (in the Queneauian sense of the phrase) of our podcast
series *Out of the Past: Investigating Film Noir* to generate the "investigative notes" accompanying each noireme; that is, all the observations and commentaries in this text originally took form in a spoken format. From the beginning of our podcasting project, we

considered the podcasts to be a new form of scholarship, and we wanted to make that case in this book.[2] Through constraint, we were able to change each "dictum" from the podcast into a "transcriptum"—*mutatis mutandis,* as Perec put it in his Post-scriptum to *A Void.*[3]

The word *transcriptum* literally means "to write across, beyond or through." In its most common English derivative, "transcription," such a writing practice implies an unerring fidelity to the original proceedings, as in transcribing a legal matter or a lecture. While we felt a need to "respect" the original expressions from the podcasts, we did not want to just "write across" from podcast to book, leaving literal transcripts of what we said in another medium.

But the many senses of *transcriptum,* and our understanding and appreciation of oulipian constraint, helped us circumvent such literal transcription. We established for ourselves, as a means to stimulate the creative and critical process, a series of simple constraints governing how we could "write through" or "write beyond" the original dicta of the podcasts. These constraints respected the original nature of the expressions (as part of a sustained and scholarly oral discourse), while at the same time making them appropriate for a new writerly context:

- We could add one sentence at the beginning or end of the text block, by way of introduction or conclusion (this constitutes an additional level of constraint).
- We could add or clarify actor, character, or crew names.
- We could delete extraneous comments.
- We could make very minor corrections (grammatical, syntactical, or historical).
- We could remove or clarify parts of sentences that made sense within spoken conversation but were unnecessary or inadequately defined in written form.
- We could resequence phrases or sentences to give a written flow.
- In a truly oulipian fashion, we would very occasionally violate these constraints if by doing so we achieved a superior result—one that demonstrated an understanding of the constraint, and how and why it was appropriate to . . . well, cheat it a little.[4]

Ultimately, we had to change little to respect these constraints, for we had spoken the essential insights. It was, as we've said, a matter of rendering the dictum as a *transcriptum* —*mutatis mutandis* (mostly). We would encourage readers of this book to listen back to our podcasts to investigate how the former gave rise to the later, how the constraints governed and stimulated that transformation, and to hear further thoughts and commentaries that did not make it onto these pages.

The Guilty Parties

Out of the Past: Investigating Film Noir

WHEN WE UNDERTOOK our shared inquiry into film noir, our goals were both modest and grand: modest in that we wanted a simple method for capturing our nascent dialogue on the topic of film noir, grand in that we thought from the start our approach might constitute a new form of scholarship in the digital age. We wanted to turn our conversations on film noir into scholarly work that captured the spontaneity of our exchanges but could be archived and peer warranted—an investigation that would produce quick results but let us retrace our steps in reflective ways. We settled on podcasting our dialogue at regular intervals. *The Maltese Touch of Evil* (a textual product) emerged from a spoken practice, published as episodes of our podcast series *Out of the Past: Investigating Film Noir.*

Podcasting takes its name from Apple's now omnipresent MP3 device the iPod, and the practice involves the creation and sharing of digital audio content by means of networked multimedia devices such as iPods, cell phones, and computers. Podcasts emerged as part of Web 2.0 culture focused on user-generated content, and they can be produced easily on any computer with a microphone and audio editing software. A podcast is delivered via the Web using RSS syndication,[1] which allows listeners to subscribe to a podcast so they automatically receive new episodes directly to their computer. Podcasting's popularity grew with the creation of "podcatchers" (software tools that aggregate and collect information on podcasts) and online podcast directories that operate as websites, both of which made podcasts easy for listeners to locate. Because podcasts are so easy to produce, distribute, and access, a DIY (do it yourself) aesthetic reigns in podcasting.

Precisely because the technology is simple, the practical uses of the technology multiply. From the beginning, we conceived of our podcasts as a new form of electronic publication: the "serialized academic audiobook." Instead of writing down our insights into noir, we speak them into a microphone, then edit our dialogue into a digital audio file. We published the first episode of *Out of the Past: Investigating Film Noir* in July 2005, continued to publish a new installment to this series every month until June 2008, and still publish new episodes periodically. Each episode of the podcast series (which taken as a whole constitutes our serialized academic audiobook) examines a single film noir or neo-noir in depth, and the typical episode lasts approximately thirty to thirty-five minutes.

Our first episode investigated Jacques Tourneur's 1947 noir classic *Out of the Past*. We took the name of that film as the title of the podcast series because it seemed to us that noir aesthetics were creeping back into Hollywood films in the climate of the War on Terror, perhaps because the United States was anxious in many of the ways it had been during and following World War II—the classic era of noir. This was something of a working hypothesis that grounded our investigations.

By many measures, especially in terms of their popular reach, the podcasts have been very successful.[2] As of August 2011, the moment we are revising this postliminary, they have generated over 480,000 downloads—in every continent but Antarctica—and continue to generate approximately 5,000 new downloads per month.[3] For a project conceived as academic scholarship, an audience of this size is surprising and gratifying.

Additionally, fans, professors, and students routinely write to say our insights into these films help them to better understand noir, while at the same time challenging many of their assumptions about its history, features, and boundaries. The podcasts have been assigned as part of a podcasting workshop in higher education, where they are cited as exemplary acts of "public intellectual" work,[4] are currently referenced in a Wikipedia article on the film *Murder, My Sweet* and cited under the topic "film noir,"[5] and are finding their way into the syllabi of college films courses.

We are not, however, writing this postliminary because we want to share our satisfaction with the project. Rather, we want to understand why these podcasts have found an audience within and beyond academia, consider the value of such a broad purview, and argue that innovative scholarship such as the serialized academic audiobook constitutes publication that should be recognized and rewarded by the academy.

We suspected from the outset that generating podcasts as scholarship might be misunderstood and would be controversial in the academy, since humanities scholarship has long-standing and well-codified processes of review and reward. Nonetheless, we felt a new method of inquiry was needed to achieve new insights into these films, and our "little man" was telling us that, if we just went with that gut feeling, the product of our investigations would evidence intellectual engagement of a scope and intensity to satisfy the scrutiny of Rank and Tenure.

Like most meaningful collaborations, this one was the product of what seemed to be a chance encounter but was really anything but. We were offered assistant professorships at the same small liberal arts college at the same time.[6] There we met and discovered we'd accepted our posts for many of the same reasons. We were attracted to the four-semester Great Books Seminar sequence, which all undergraduate students were required to take and all faculty to teach. We both suspected that, in working with professors and students forced out of their disciplines by the seminar, we would achieve a greater understanding of the very process of learning and would be better able to chart and follow the diverse constellation of interests that guided our own scholarship.

In that environment the podcast took form, and its form is largely a testament to that environment. We conceived of the podcast not only as a means of investigating our shared love of noir but also as a way of modeling what we considered to be good seminar conversation. That conversation is always rooted in the text, yet possesses unusual extratextual powers, as described by Roland Barthes in his essay "To the Seminar":

> The seminar assumes responsibility for . . . writing a book (by a montage of writings) . . . it regards its own—non-functional—practice as already constituting a text: the

rarest text, one which does not appear in writing. A certain way of being together can fulfill the inscription of significance . . . there are texts which are not products but practices. (1989b, 333)

Our conversations about film noir were exactly such a "text as practice." However, the simple technology of podcasting left a record of this previously ephemeral sort of text. Moreover, the experience of podcasting and leading seminar in the classroom during the same academic year created an interesting mirroring effect. We were able to see each of these parallel pursuits reflected in the other, and thereby to gain a certain critical perspective on both.

We were first struck by the ways the Great Books seem to be active participants in all discussions that surround them. They have the uncommon ability to both frame themselves and signal to us that our reading frames them. At its best, seminar conversation is aware of this; it comprehends that the texts don't need our intervention in order to be significant, yet as we read them we add something to them and to our understanding of ourselves—of how and why they, and we, make meaning. As a result, both readings and reading methodologies grow from the primary sources. To take the argument slightly further, and put it in terms more familiar to scholars, the Great Books—by virtue of the extreme care with which they are constructed, a care that demonstrates a rare degree of self-consciousness—at once script auto-exegesis and beg us to recognize that our exegeses of them work from existing, and establish new, interpretive paradigms that rescript them.

As we continued work on the podcasts, it became clear to us that great films noir have the same bifurcated power. Our initial understanding of the podcast series—as a "certain way of being together" to investigate a shared interest in noir and to model seminar behavior—came to seem too narrow. The investigation was neither ephemeral nor grounded uniquely (even primarily) in pedagogical concerns. Rather, it had quickly become a critical examination of noir that inscribed our thoughts on how noir engaged with the great historical, economic, and philosophical crises of the years 1941–1958, as well as how noir interacted quite self-consciously with film history and the very medium of film.

In other words, the investigation had quickly outgrown its institutional and pedagogical foundations to become a form of scholarly inquiry, and the podcasts had much in common with other academic publications. While they were structured differently from most academic publications, they were nonetheless precisely that. Each episode contained at least one, and often several, new insights into the film it investigated. Like articles, each was an installment in a book in progress that could be peer warranted.

We presented this position during the New Media Consortium's Online Conference on Personal Broadcasting, in a talk entitled "Podcasting as Publication: Constructing a Serialized Academic Audiobook."[7] It was well received—considered both plausible and provocative. We likewise presented the argument to the Rank and Tenure committee at our institution, where it was received with reservations.[8]

This cautious response was expected and was ultimately a boon. It forced us to give further thought to the particular merits of our form of scholarship and led us to consider how our insights could be translated to print. We had to address not only *what* we were fashioning in terms of scholarship but also *how* we were fashioning it. We hope the original podcast series (text as practice) and this book (text as product) will challenge assumptions about what academic publications should look like and do.

Inevitably, we brought to the project bits of scaffolding from our former studies: Edwards had examined political and progressive uses of new media while earning a PhD in critical studies from University of Southern California's School of Cinema-Television; Clute had studied the critical effects of self-conscious punning and intertextual borrowing while earning a PhD in romance studies from Cornell University. But we did not want our podcasts to alternate between the two disciplinary framings, or favor one approach over another. We sought a transdisciplinary approach that would privilege the primary sources while valuing the training we had received—keeping us alert to the opportunities born of understanding, and benefiting from, one another's disciplinary and theoretical orientations.

The act of transliterating the podcasts into this manuscript alerted us to the pitfalls of superficial interdisciplinarity. We had undertaken the podcasts out of shared intellectual passion and a desire to read the "texts" as best we could, discuss them, and see what came of it. But as our insights went to print (and underwent blind review), it was evident scholars would want to frame our work through certain disciplinary lenses that didn't capture our project. By enacting what we dubbed "close readings" in the podcast series, it was never our intention to propose a *new* New Criticism, nor were we adopting seminar reading protocols out of an intellectual nostalgia for a bygone academic era.

In fact, what we were practicing was a very particular sort of close reading exercise, one that did not shy away from the language or insights of critical theory that were part of our intellectual training, but always started with, and largely privileged, the "source text" (i.e., the film). Our close readings were critical reflections born of the films, lenses projected by the films that reflected back upon those films (or could be easily and unobtrusively positioned to do). By focusing on the films themselves in the context of a deeply interdisciplinary dialogue, we were forced to consider two truths of our project: we strove to counter our natural tendencies to frame readings of film noir through our respective disciplines; the better we got at avoiding disciplinary readings, the more clearly we saw how these films, like great books, structured frames through which we found ourselves reading them.

In essence, we had moved beyond superficial interdisciplinarity and were exploring what W. J. T. Mitchell would call the "indiscipline" of film studies:

"Indiscipline" is a moment of breakage or rupture, when the continuity is broken and the practice comes into question. To be sure this moment of rupture can itself become routinized, as the rapid transformation of deconstruction from an "event" into a "method of interpretation" demonstrates. When the tigers break into the temple and profane the altar too regularly, their appearance rapidly becomes part of the sacred ritual. Nevertheless, there is that moment before the routine or ritual is reasserted, the moment of chaos or wonder when a discipline, a way of doing things, compulsively performs a revelation of its own inadequacy. This is the moment of interdisciplinarity that has always interested me. (1995, 541)

In hindsight, we can see our podcast efforts as "profaning the altar" of peer-reviewed scholarship, as if we were "tigers" breaking into the temple with a new form of publication.[9]

More importantly, Mitchell's comments underscore what made our podcasts interesting to us and so difficult to translate into a manuscript: the outcome of any given discussion was not certain. Both in the podcasts and in this text we wanted to do work so interdisciplinary it constituted "indiscipline." In the case of podcasting, that was relatively easy. Each of us watched each film in isolation and prepared for our recording session in isolation. When recording started, we did not know what the other person was going to say or what the ultimate direction of the podcast would be. Asking one another questions led down pathways we had not even considered when we started recording, or sometimes led to moments of incoherence or turbulence as we sought to respond. Our very method forced us to drop our disciplinary guards because it was crucial, in real time, that we understand each other. It was a collegial dialogue, a system of analytical give and take, that performed the revelation of the inadequacy of each discipline.

While many scholars are able to dismantle disciplinary boundaries in their pedagogy or public speaking engagements, they tend to build them up in their publication (a practice frequently oriented toward a specialized audience), to the point these boundaries become impenetrable constructions to those outside that disciplinary temple. The challenge we faced was to find a physical form and critical framework for our written text that would duplicate the flexibility of the conversations and allow for unanticipated insights. We needed a form of written indiscipline that maintained the moment of chaos and wonder by not allowing it to become fixed. So it is that we struck upon the methodology outlined above.

Before there is an investigation, there is a story of something that has happened. In a nutshell, this is ours.

Computers and Writers

The MTOE Project

This project [A.R.T.A.] is of triple interest: first, it allows for the production of stories, which is nice when one likes that; second, it allows for the elaboration, in prudent little steps, of a unique grammar; third, it allows for the establishment of a stock of agms that may be used on other occasions, but that is an arduous project that is only beginning. It will take patience, work, and time (=money). (translation ours)

—Paul Fournel, "Computer and Writer: The Centre Pompidou Experiment"[1]

The book read by each reader is always another book.

—Italo Calvino, "How I Wrote One of My Books"

If the previous postliminary looked at how this book can be traced back to a podcast out of our past, then this postliminary looks forward to how the project might evolve in a digital future.

This book is part of a digital logics progression that blurs previous distinctions between forms of scholarship: the podcast as a serialized audiobook, this book as recombinatorial text, a (potential) potential database as means to generate serialized recombinatorics, and so forth. Each iteration of this project engages in a digital poetics that privileges converging and transmedia-inspired content (even while various scholarly forms will likely retain their specialized and distinct qualities for some time to come). While we cannot predict future technologies, nor anticipate what new forms of the continuing inquiry into noir and potential criticism they will enable, we propose one potential version of future remediation of our study—the MTOE Project (an acronym for "Maltese Touch of Evil" Project), a participatory, procedural (and ultimately, perhaps, encyclopedic) database dedicated to film noir.[2]

At the outset, we should say that the digital humanities logics driving the MTOE Project have (of course) already been plagiarized by anticipation by members of the Oulipo. Italo Calvino's famous lecture on the role of cybernetics in the study of literature, "Cybernetics and Ghosts," dates back to 1968, and the A.R.T.A. Project (which stands for "Atelier de Recherches et Techniques Avancées," or "Workshop of Advanced Studies and Techniques") has been exploring computer-based analyses of literature for over three decades. In the twenty-first century, more and more scholars will be turning toward the digital humanities as part of their writing and research (including utilizing digital tools and digital publishing), and oulipian methods are likely to motivate and shape such experiments and their resultant products—or so they should.[3]

The MTOE Project would start by building a multifunctional database of noiremes to support the activities of online film noir communities. Given that the database would be in a digital format, the potential would exist to add more than still images, and a robust version of this idea would seek to allow sound and video clips.[4] Moreover the MTOE Project would allow readers to add their own investigative notes, to tag or annotate the filmic material with further information and metadata, to author new noiremes, and to suggest or create constraints for resequencing existing noiremes (percent of a frame in shadow, number of times "Baby" is uttered in one scene of a screenplay, etc.) to aid further synoulipistic and anoulipistic investigations into film noir.[5] As is the case with the A.R.T.A. Project, the greatest benefits would be born of computers aiding the reader to engage in multiple and unanticipated ways with the texts. The MTOE Project would be fully oulipian in that it would be designed to be a "creation that creates" (*création crééante*) new analyses of existing films noir and new noir narratives (or even noir films).

The role of the reader would be decisive in such a database. In fact, readers would always be, in some sense, the authors of the MTOE Project. This is in keeping with the procedural and participatory logics of digital networks and oulipian sewing circles. Clearly, *The Maltese Touch of Evil* manuscript is a precursor to the MTOE Project, and in its methodology—from podcast dictums to print transcriptums—it evinces and invites the collaborative ethos characteristic of the aforementioned communities.

The key distinction between *The Maltese Touch of Evil* and the MTOE Project is that the latter would facilitate the addition of supplements and would allow each contributor to frame comments in his or her own words rather than relying on the "authors" to do that work. Indeed, as is true of the oulipian "ouvroir," the MTOE Project would make authors of all who work through the given constraints (or new ones of their invention).[6] Like any meaningful collaboration, the MTOE Project would problematize and democratize the very concept of authorship. The idea is to expand the sewing circle in order to embroider a larger tapestry of noir. The potential of such a digitally accessible *ouvroir* is immense and could prove immensely satisfying—with fans, scholars, and filmmakers coming together to share their love and knowledge of film noir.

Selected Filmography

Here is the alphabetical list of the films from which the noiremes were selected. These credits are based on information provided by the Internet Movie Database (www.imdb .com/), as verified in April 2010.

The Asphalt Jungle (1950)

Studio:	Metro-Goldwyn-Mayer (MGM)
DVD:	Burbank, Calif.: Turner Entertainment and Warner Bros., 2004
Director:	John Huston
Screenplay:	Ben Maddow and John Huston, based on the novel by W. R. Burnett
Cinematographer:	Harold Rosson
Cast:	Sterling Hayden: Dix Handley
	Louis Calhern: Alonzo D. Emmerich
	Jean Hagen: Doll Conovan
	James Whitmore: Gus Minissi
	Sam Jaffe: Doc Erwin Riedenschneider
Running Time:	112 minutes
Noiremes:	002: An Imbalanced World
	014: A City in Ruins
	043: City and Country
	060: The Players
	068: Time and Crime
	100: Deadly Nostalgia

Batman Begins (2005)

Studio:	Warner Bros.
DVD:	Burbank, Calif.: Warner Bros., 2005
Director:	Christopher Nolan
Screenplay:	Christopher Nolan and David S. Goyer, based on a story by David S. Goyer
Cinematographer:	Wally Pfister
Cast:	Christian Bale: Bruce Wayne/Batman
	Michael Caine: Alfred

Liam Neeson: Henri Ducard
Katie Holmes: Rachel Dawes
Gary Oldman: Jim Gordon

Running Time:	140 minutes
Noiremes:	029: Gotham Cities
	086: Terror in the City

The Big Lebowski (1998)

Studio:	Polygram Filmed Entertainment
DVD:	Universal City, Calif.: Universal Studios, 2005 (Collector's Edition)
Director:	Joel Coen
Screenplay:	Ethan Coen and Joel Coen
Cinematographer:	Roger Deakins
Cast:	Jeff Bridges: The Dude
	John Goodman: Walter Sobchak
	Julianne Moore: Maude Lebowski
	Steve Buscemi: Donny
	David Huddleston: Jeffrey Lebowski
Running Time:	117 minutes
Noiremes:	079: Defective Detective Work
	081: A License to Hallucinate

The Big Sleep (1946)

Studio:	Warner Bros.
DVD:	Burbank, Calif.: Warner Bros., 1997
Director:	Howard Hawks
Screenplay:	William Faulkner, Leigh Brackett, and Jules Furthman, based on the novel by Raymond Chandler
Cinematographer:	Sidney Hickox
Cast:	Humphrey Bogart: Philip Marlowe
	Lauren Bacall: Vivian Rutledge
	Martha Vickers: Carmen Sternwood
	Dorothy Malone: Acme Book Shop Proprietress
	Charles Waldron: General Sternwood
Running Time:	114 minutes
Noiremes:	023: Let Him Sweat
	036: Noir Entrendres
	044: A Rub of the Ear
	101: Cleaning Endings

Blade Runner: Director's Cut (1982; 1992)

Studio:	Warner Bros.
DVD:	Burbank, Calif.: Warner Bros., 1997 (Ultimate Collector's Edition)
Director:	Ridley Scott
Screenplay:	Hampton Fancher and David Peoples, based on the novel *Do Androids Dream of Electric Sheep?* by Philip K. Dick
Cinematographer:	Jordan Cronenweth
Cast:	Harrison Ford: Rick Deckard
	Rutger Hauer: Roy Batty
	Sean Young: Rachael
	Edward James Olmos: Gaff
	Daryl Hannah: Pris
Running Time:	116 minutes
Noiremes:	016: Down to Earth
	031: Looking Back and Looking Ahead
	040: The Lie is in the Eye

Chinatown (1974)

Studio:	Paramount Pictures
DVD:	Hollywood, Calif.: Paramount Pictures, 1999 (Widescreen Collection)
Director:	Roman Polanski
Screenplay:	Robert Towne
Cinematographer:	John A. Alonzo
Cast:	Jack Nicholson: J. J. Gittes
	Faye Dunaway: Evelyn Mulwray
	John Huston: Noah Cross
	Darrell Zwerling: Hollis Mulwray
Running Time:	131 minutes
Noiremes:	010: Noir Color
	025: Point of View
	058: Florsheim Shoe
	094: The Dreams Made of Stuff

Detour (1945)

Studio:	Producers Releasing Corporation (PRC)
DVD:	Woodland Hills, Calif.: St. Clair Entertainment Group, 2007
Director:	Edgar G. Ulmer
Screenplay:	Martin Goldsmith
Cinematographer:	Benjamin H. Kline

Cast:	Tom Neal: Al Roberts
	Ann Savage: Vera
	Claudia Drake: Sue Harvey
	Edmund MacDonald: Charles Haskell Jr.
Running Time:	67 minutes
Noiremes:	022: Looking into Noir

D.O.A. (1950)

Studio:	United Artists
DVD:	Woodland Hills, Calif.: St. Clair Entertainment Group, 2007
Director:	Rudolph Maté
Screenplay:	Russell Rouse and Clarence Green
Cinematographer:	Ernest Laszlo
Cast:	Edmond O'Brien: Frank Bigelow
	Pamela Britton: Paul Gibson
	Luther Adler: Majak
	Beverly Garland: Miss Foster
Running Time:	83 minutes
Noiremes:	004: The Man in Charge
	063: Life Issues

Double Indemnity (1944)

Studio:	Paramount Pictures
DVD:	Universal City, Calif.: Universal Studios, 2006 (Universal Legacy Series)
Director:	Billy Wilder
Screenplay:	Billy Wilder and Raymond Chandler, based on the novel by James M. Cain
Cinematographer:	John Seitz
Cast:	Fred MacMurray: Walter Neff
	Barbara Stanwyck: Phyllis Dietrichson
	Edward G. Robinson: Barton Keyes
Running Time:	107 minutes
Noiremes:	021: Smack Up Against Your Nose
	033: Show, Don't Tell
	054: Wearing the Pants

Good Night, and Good Luck (2005)

Studio:	Warner Independent Pictures
DVD:	Burbank, Calif.: Warner Bros., 2005
Director:	George Clooney
Screenplay:	George Clooney and Grant Heslov

Cinematographer: Robert Elswit
Cast: David Strathairn: Edward R. Murrow
                  George Clooney: Fred Friendly
                  Jeff Daniels: Sig Mickelson
                  Frank Langella: William Paley
                  Patricia Clarkson: Shirley Wershba
                  Robert Downey Jr.: Joe Wershba
Running Time: 93 minutes
Noiremes: 027: The News on Noir
                  047: Closing In

The Grifters (1990)

Studio: Miramax Films
DVD: New York: HBO Home Video, 1998
Director: Stephen Frears
Screenplay: Donald E. Westlake, based on the novel by Jim Thompson
Cinematographer: Oliver Stapleton
Cast: Angelica Huston: Lilly Dillon
                  John Cusack: Roy Dillon
                  Annette Bening: Myra Langtry
Running Time: 110 minutes
Noiremes: 019: Vertical Bars
                  030: A Hard Blow to the Guts
                  035: Smack
                  095: Going Down

Gun Crazy (1950)

Studio: United Artists
DVD: Burbank, Calif.: Warner Bros., 2004
Director: Joseph H. Lewis
Screenplay: MacKinlay Kantor and Dalton Trumbo
                  (under the front Millard Kaufman)
Cinematographer: Russell Harlan
Cast: John Dall: Bart Tare
                  Peggy Cummins: Annie Starr
                  Berry Kroeger: Packett
                  Mickey Little: Bart Tare (age 7)
                  Russ Tamblyn: Bart Tare (age 14)
Running Time: 86 minutes
Noiremes: 011: Needing a Gun
                  020: Childhood Ain't Pretty
                  048: Ecstatic Shots

059: Noir Camp
083: Roller Coaster
102: This Fog-shrouded World

He Walked by Night (1948)

Studio:	Eagle-Lion Films
DVD:	Santa Monica, Calif.: MGM Home Entertainment, 2003
Director:	Alfred L. Werker (and Anthony Mann, uncredited)
Screenplay:	Crane Wilbur and John C. Higgins, based on a story by Crane Wilbur
Cinematographer:	John Alton
Cast:	Richard Basehart: Roy Morgan
	Scott Brady: Sgt. Marty Brennan
	Roy Roberts: Capt. Breen
	Jack Webb: Lee Whitey
Running Time:	79 minutes
Noiremes:	041: A War of Procedures
	070: Assembling the Picture
	089: Lights Out
	091: In the Sewers

The Hitch-Hiker (1953)

Studio:	RKO Radio Pictures
DVD:	Woodland Hills, Calif.: St. Clair Entertainment Group, 2007
Director:	Ida Lupino
Screenplay:	Collier Young and Ida Lupino (with uncredited writing by Daniel Mainwaring)
Cinematographer:	Nicholas Musuraca
Cast:	Edmond O'Brien: Roy Collins
	Frank Lovejoy: Gilbert Bowen
	William Talman: Emmett Myers
Running Time:	71 minutes
Noiremes:	006: To the Point
	028: The Random Element
	057: Defective Oversight

It's a Wonderful Life (1946)

Studio:	Liberty Films/RKO Radio Pictures
DVD:	Hollywood, Calif.: Paramount Studios, 2006
Director:	Frank Capra
Screenplay:	Frances Goodrich, Albert Hackett, and Frank Capra, based on a story by Philip Van Doren Stern

Cinematographers: Joseph F. Biroc and Joseph Walker
Cast: James Stewart: George Bailey
                         Donna Reed: Mary Hatch Bailey
                         Lionel Barrymore: Henry Potter
                         Thomas Mitchell: Uncle Billy
                         Henry Travers: Clarence
Running Time: 130 minutes
Noiremes: 082: A Dead Dream and a Deaf Ear
                         088: The Fall of Bedford Falls

The Killers (1946)

Studio: Universal Pictures
DVD: The Criterion Collection, 2003
Director: Robert Siodmak
Screenplay: Anthony Veiller, based on the story by Ernest Hemingway
Cinematographer: Woody Bredell
Cast: Burt Lancaster: Swede Andersen
                   Ava Gardner: Kitty Collins
                   Edmond O'Brien: Jim Reardon
                   Vince Barnett: Charleston
Running Time: 103 minutes
Noiremes: 003: Moving Too Fast
                   034: A Frenchman's Question and The Swede's Answer
                   049: Money Is No Insurance
                   073: The Golden Harps
                   076: The Mirror and the Blind Man

The Killing (1956)

Studio: United Artists
DVD: Santa Monica, Calif.: MGM Home Entertainment, 1999
Director: Stanley Kubrick
Screenplay: Stanley Kubrick, based on the novel *Clean Break* by Lionel White,
                   with dialogue by Jim Thompson
Cinematographer: Lucien Ballard
Cast: Sterling Hayden: Johnny Clay
                   Coleen Gray: Fay
                   Vince Edwards: Val Cannon
                   Jay C. Flippen: Marvin Unger
                   Elisha Cook Jr.: George Peatty
                   Marie Windsor: Sherry Peatty
Running Time: 85 minutes
Noiremes: 026: Voice of God

055: The Academy of Chumps and Suckers
090: Not Fair
096: The Probability of a Poodle

Kiss Me Deadly (1955)

Studio:	United Artists
DVD:	Santa Monica, Calif.: MGM Home Entertainment, 2001
Director:	Robert Aldrich
Screenplay:	A. I. Bezzerides, based on the novel by Mickey Spillane
Cinematographer:	Ernest Laszlo
Cast:	Ralph Meeker: Mike Hammer
	Maxine Cooper: Velda
	Cloris Leachman: Christina Bailey
	Paul Stewart: Carl Evello
Running Time:	106 minutes
Noiremes:	005: The Erotic and the Neurotic
	042: Look Deep
	072: LA Absurd
	085: The Hammering Hero
	097: Irresistible Danger

The Lady from Shanghai (1947)

Studio:	Columbia Pictures
DVD:	Culver City, Calif.: Columbia TriStar Home Video, 2000
Director:	Orson Welles
Screenplay:	Orson Welles, based on the novel *If I Die before I Wake* by Sherwood King
Cinematographer:	Charles Lawton Jr.
Cast:	Rita Hayworth: Elsa Bannister
	Orson Welles: Michael O'Hara
	Everett Sloane: Arthur Bannister
	Glenn Anders: George Grisby
Running Time:	87 minutes
Noiremes:	012: Cut and Dyed
	074: Sharks in the Water
	084: On Trial

Laura (1944)

Studio:	Twentieth Century Fox
DVD:	Beverly Hills, Calif.: Twentieth Century Fox Home Entertainment, 2004
Director:	Otto Preminger

Screenplay:	Jay Dratler, Samuel Hoffenstein, and Betty Reinhardt, based on the novel by Vera Caspary
Cinematographer:	Joseph LaShelle
Cast:	Gene Tierney: Laura Hunt
	Dana Andrews: Det. Lt. Mark McPherson
	Clifton Webb: Waldo Lydecker
	Vincent Price: Shelby Carpenter
Running Time:	88 minutes
Noiremes:	038: Noir Atmosphere
	075: Playing with the Theme
	078: Undercover
	080: Under a Harsh Glare

The Maltese Falcon (1941)

Studio:	Warner Bros.
DVD:	Burbank, Calif.: Warner Home Video, 2000
Director:	John Huston
Screenplay:	John Huston, based on the novel by Dashiell Hammett
Cinematographer:	Arthur Edeson
Cast:	Humphrey Bogart: Sam Spade
	Mary Astor: Brigid O'Shaughnessy
	Peter Lorre: Joel Cairo
	Sydney Greenstreet: Kasper Gutman
	Elisha Cook Jr.: Wilmer Cook
Running Time:	101 minutes
Noiremes:	024: Time for a New Protagonist
	032: The Upper Hand
	066: A Flutter of Curtains
	099: The Stuff Dreams Are Made Of

The Man Who Wasn't There (2001)

Studio:	Working Title Films/Good Machine International
DVD:	Universal City, Calif.: Universal Studios, 2002
Director:	Joel Coen
Screenplay:	Ethan Coen and Joel Coen
Cinematographer:	Roger Deakins
Cast:	Billy Bob Thornton: Ed Crane
	Frances McDormand: Doris Crane
	Michael Badalucco: Frank
	James Gandolfini: Big Dave Brewster
	Katherine Borowitz: Ann Nirdlinger Brewster
	Jon Polito: Creighton Tolliver
	Scarlett Johansson: Birdy Abundas

Running Time: 116 minutes
Noiremes: 046: In Between Meaning

Murder, My Sweet (1944)

Studio: RKO Radio Pictures
DVD: Burbank, Calif.: Warner Bros., 2004
Director: Edward Dmytryk
Screenplay: John Paxton, based on the novel *Farewell, My Lovely* by Raymond Chandler
Cinematographer: Harry J. Wild
Cast: Dick Powell: Philip Marlowe
Claire Trevor: Helen Grayle/Velma Valento
Ann Shirley: Ann Grayle
Otto Kruger: Jules Amthor
Mike Mazurki: Moose Malloy
Running Time: 95 Minutes
Noiremes: 013: The Blind Man's View
017: Shots in the City
051: Chandler's Marlowe
052: Powell's Marlowe
067: Noir in the Head

Notorious (1946)

Studio: RKO Radio Pictures
DVD: Beverly Hills, Calif.: Starz/Anchor Bay, 1999
Director: Alfred Hitchcock
Screenplay: Ben Hecht
Cinematographer: Ted Tetzlaff
Cast: Cary Grant: T. R. Devlin
Ingrid Bergman: Alicia Huberman
Claude Rains: Alexander Sebastian
Louis Calhern: Captain Paul Prescott
Running Time: 101 Minutes
Noiremes: 015: Noir Shoots Stars

On the Waterfront (1954)

Studio: Columbia Pictures
DVD: Culver City, Calif.: Sony Pictures, 2001 (Special Edition)
Director: Elia Kazan
Screenplay: Budd Schulberg, based on his story
Cinematographer: Boris Kaufman
Cast: Marlon Brando: Terry Malloy
Karl Malden: Father Barry

Lee J. Cobb: Johnny Friendly
Rod Steiger: Charley Malloy
Eva Marie Saint: Edie Doyle

Running Time:	108 minutes
Noiremes:	064: The Flipside of Noir
	071: Artful and Artless

Out of the Past (1947)

Studio:	RKO Radio Pictures
DVD:	Burbank, Calif.: Warner Bros. Entertainment, 2004
Director:	Jacques Tourneur
Screenplay:	Daniel Mainwaring
Cinematographer:	Nicholas Musuraca
Cast:	Robert Mitchum: Jeff Bailey
	Jane Greer: Kathie Moffat
	Kirk Douglas: Whit Sterling
Running Time:	97 minutes
Noiremes:	008: Into the Countryside
	053: Caught

The Postman Always Rings Twice (1946)

Studio:	Metro-Goldwyn-Mayer (MGM)
DVD:	Burbank, Calif.: Warner Bros. Entertainment, 2004
Director:	Tay Garnett
Screenplay:	Harry Ruskin and Niven Busch, based on the novel by James M. Cain
Cinematographer:	Sidney Wagner
Cast:	Lana Turner: Cora Smith
	John Garfield: Frank Chambers
	Cecil Kellaway: Nick Smith
	Hume Cronyn: Arthur Keats
Running Time:	113 minutes
Noiremes:	018: Glamour Noir
	037: Open Is Closed
	077: Framed

Du rififi chez les hommes (Rififi) (1955)

Studio:	Pathé Consortium Cinéma
DVD:	The Criterion Collection, 2001
Director:	Jules Dassin
Screenplay:	Jules Dassin, based on the novel by Auguste Le Breton
Cinematographer:	Philippe Agostini

Cast:	Jean Servais: Tony le Stéphanois
	Carl Möhner: Jo le Suedois
	Robert Manuel: Mario Ferrati
	Janine Darcey: Louise le Suedois
Running Time:	122 minutes
Noiremes:	045: Luscious Collisions
	061: Silenced

The Set-Up (1949)

Studio:	RKO Radio Pictures
DVD:	Burbank, Calif.: Warner Bros. Entertainment, 2004
Director:	Robert Wise
Screenplay:	Art Cohn, based on the poem by Joseph Moncure March
Cinematographer:	Milton R. Krasner
Cast:	Robert Ryan: Stoker Thompson
	Audrey Totter: Julie
	George Tobias: Tiny
	Alan Baxter: Little Boy
	Wallace Ford: Gus
Running Time:	72 minutes
Noiremes:	009: Running Out of Time
	093: Downbeat

Sunset Blvd. (1950)

Studio:	Paramount Pictures
DVD:	Hollywood, Calif.: Paramount Home Video, 2002
Director:	Billy Wilder
Screenplay:	Charles Brackett, Billy Wilder, and D. M. Marshman Jr.
Cinematographer:	John F. Seitz
Cast:	William Holden: Joe Gillis
	Gloria Swanson: Norma Desmond
	Erich von Stroheim: Max Von Mayerling
	Nancy Olson: Betty Schaefer
Running Time:	110 minutes
Noiremes:	001: In the Gutter
	050: Nooses and Nets
	056: Car Trouble
	098: The Staircase

Touch of Evil (1958 [Restoration Version, 1998])

| Studio: | Universal International Pictures |
| DVD: | Universal City, Calif.: Universal Studios, 2000 |

Director:	Orson Welles
Screenplay:	Orson Welles, based on the novel *Badge of Evil* by Whit Masterson
Cinematographer:	Russell Metty
Restoration:	Walter Murch (editing), Bob O'Neil (Universal's director of film restoration), and Bill Varney (sound engineer), based on fifty-eight-page memo from Orson Welles
Restoration Producer:	Rick Schmidlin
Cast:	Charlton Heston: Ramon Miguel "Mike" Vargas
	Janet Leigh: Susie Vargas
	Orson Welles: Hank Quinlan
	Joseph Calleia: Pete Menzies
	Akim Tamiroff: Uncle Joe Grandi
	Dennis Weaver: Mirador Motel Night Manager
Running Time:	95 minutes [1958]; 112 minutes [1998 restoration version]
Noiremes:	007: Blowing Up Noir
	039: We're Closed
	062: Stealing from the Blind
	065: Doubled, Crossed
	069: Upon Reflection
	087: A Bull Outside the Ring
	092: The Slightest Separation

Podcastography

Out of the Past: Investigating Film Noir podcasts are online at the iTunes Music Store and at http://outofthepast.libsyn.com/.

Out of the Past is produced, written, and hosted by Shannon Clute and Richard Edwards. *Out of the Past* is a scholarly podcast, and its episodes can be searched using World-Cat, the world's largest library catalog (www.worldcat.org/).

Episode 50: *The Blue Dahlia*
Published: 11/7/2009

Episode 49: *Bande à part/Band of Outsiders* (with Dr. Jeffrey Peters)
Published: 8/24/2009

Episode 48: *In a Lonely Place* (with Megan Abbott)
Published: 12/27/2008

Episode 47: *Bob le Flambeur* (with Howard Rodman and Mike White)
Published: 8/12/2008

Episode 46: *Thieves' Highway* (with Eddie Muller)
Published: 6/18/2008

Episode 45: *Force of Evil*
Published: 3/11/2008

Episode 44: *Brick*
Published: 2/5/2008

Episode 43: *They Live by Night*
Published: 1/3/2008

Episode 42: *Ice Harvest* (with Scott Phillips)
Published: 12/5/2007

Episode 41: *The Glass Key* and *Miller's Crossing* (Coen Brothers Double Feature 3)
Published: 11/10/2007

Episode 40: *Gilda*
Published: 10/8/2007

Episode 39: *Kiss Kiss Bang Bang*
Published: 9/1/2007

Episode 38: *I Wake Up Screaming*
Published: 8/3/2007

Episode 37: *Body Heat*
Published: 7/6/2007

Episode 36: *His Kind of Woman*
Published: 6/12/2007

Episode 35: *Pickup on South Street*
Published: 5/11/2007

Episode 34: *The Strange Love of Martha Ivers*
Published: 4/1/2007

Episode 33: *Hollywoodland*
Published: 3/2/2007

Episode 32: *Kiss Me Deadly*
Published: 2/1/2007

Episode 31: *Touch of Evil*
Published: 1/1/2007

Episode 30: *The Postman Always Rings Twice* and *The Man Who Wasn't There*
Published: 12/1/2006

Episode 29: *Detour*
Published: 11/1/2006

Episode 28: *The Black Dahlia*
Published: 11/1/2006

Episode 27: *D.O.A.*
Published: 9/1/2006

Episode 26: *Murder, My Sweet*
Published: 6/30/2006

Episode 25: *He Walked by Night*
Published: 6/14/2006

Episode 24: *Chinatown*
Published: 5/31/2006

Episode 23: *On the Waterfront*
Published: 5/15/2006

Episode 22: *Good Night, and Good Luck*
Published: 5/1/2006

Episode 21: *Sunset Blvd.*
Published: 4/15/2006

Episode 20: *Reservoir Dogs*
Published: 4/1/2006

Episode 19: *The Killing*
Published: 3/15/2006

Episode 18: *The Set-Up*
Published: 3/1/2006

Episode 17: *Gun Crazy*
Published: 2/15/2006

Episode 16: *The Grifters*
Published: 2/1/2006

Episode 15: *The Lady from Shanghai*
Published: 1/15/2006

Episode 14: *Notorious*
Published: 1/1/2006

Episode 13: *It's a Wonderful Life*
Published: 12/15/2005

Episode 12: *Rififi*
Published: 12/1/2005

Episode 11: *The Big Sleep* and *The Big Lebowski*
Published: 11/15/2005

Episode 10: *The Killers*
Published: 11/1/2005

Episode 9: *Laura*
Published: 10/14/2005

Episode 8: *The Asphalt Jungle*
Published: 10/1/2005

Episode 7: *The Hitch-Hiker*
Published: 9/15/2005

Episode 6: *Blade Runner*
Published: 9/1/2005

Episode 5: *The Maltese Falcon*
Published: 8/15/2005

Episode 4: *The Third Man*
Published: 8/1/2005

Episode 3: *Batman Begins*
Published: 7/15/2005

Episode 2: *Double Indemnity*
Published: 7/8/2005

Episode 1: *Out of the Past*
Published: 7/2/2005

Notes

Preface

1. This citation is drawn from Warren Motte's introduction to the superb study *Oulipo: A Primer of Potential Literature* (1986, 9).

While we will occasionally offer alternatives to Motte's translations of oulipian writings—due to the fact that we have a different understanding of certain key oulipian practices—the above work is nonetheless a crucial English-language introduction to the Oulipo and to our mind one of the most nuanced studies on the subject.

2. "Ouvroir . . . flattait ce goût modeste que nous avions pour la belle ouvrage et les bonnes oeuvres: morale et beaux-art étant respectés, nous consentîmes à lier à la li l'ou."

3. Interestingly, this was our stated goal long before we realized we were engaged in oulipian activity, and that it would be more proper to consider our fellow "investigators" as fellow members of our sewing circle. Looking back some six years later, the only thing we would change about this definition is the word "unravel," which we would define now as "embroider." For more on our *Out of the Past* project, see postliminary 1.

Chapter 1: *A Void* in Film Noir Studies

1. Krutnik suggests that noir studies is overdue for "some kind of critical reckoning." As he clarifies in his introduction to *In a Lonely Place: Film Noir, Genre, Masculinity*, Krutnik, in his approach to film noir, is seeking to avoid the "rigid" and "artificial" divide between history and theory.

2. Initially, the group comprised eleven members: François Le Lionnais, Raymond Queneau, Noël Arnaud, Jacques Bens, Claude Berge, Paul Braffort, Jacques Duchateau, Latis, Jean Lescure, Jean Queval, and Albert-Marie Schmidt. Two of the most prolific, and most famous, Oulipians were invited to join shortly thereafter: Jacques Roubaud became the twelfth member in 1966; Georges Perec, the thirteenth in 1967. Perec was an active, perhaps the most active, member of the Oulipo from that time until his premature death in 1982. For a brief history of the foundation of the Oulipo, see Bénabou 2001.

3. "Toute oeuvre littéraire se construit à partir d'une inspiration (c'est du moins ce que son auteur laisse entendre) qui est tenue à s'accommoder tant bien que mal d'une série de contraintes et de procédures qui rentrent les une dans les autres comme des poupées russes. . . . L'humanité doit-elle se reposer et se contenter, sur des pensers nouveaux de faire des vers antiques? Nous ne le croyons pas. Ce que certains écrivains ont introduit dans leur manière, avec talent (voire avec génie) mais les uns occasionnellement (forgeages de mots nouveaux), d'autres avec prédilection (contrerimes), d'autres avec insistance mais

dans une seule direction (lettrisme), l'Ouvoir de Littérature Potentielle (OuLiPo) entend le faire systématiquement et scientifiquement, et au besoin en recourant aux bons offices des machines à traiter l'information."

4. And in so doing, we hope to make manifest some of the deeper reasons that the Oulipo were among the earliest experimenters in the humanities with computer-based operations and can be seen as anticipating some of the latest developments around data-base logics and recombinant poetics in the digital humanities.

5. The direct translation of the French title is "The Disappearance," but because the translation is also a lipogram in *e,* that title was not possible.

6. A lipogram is a text written without the use of a particular letter or letters. A lipo-gram in *e* contains no *e*'s in its text (or ease for its author).

7. The tendency to read all of Perec's work, and particularly the lipogrammatic form of *La disparition,* through his personal experience of loss during the Holocaust marks the predominant theme in Perecquien scholarship: perhaps inevitably, since *e* is the only vowel needed in French to spell the words "mother" and "father" ("mère" and "père"), both of whom Perec lost to World War II (see, for example, Clément 1979; LeJeune 1991; and Magoudi 1996). Even those studies of larger scope, which examine Perec's poetics, his particular linguistic play, and his unique humor, have a tendency to conclude by viewing all of these characteristics of his work through a historical optic, often seeing his life's oeuvre above all as "autobiographie" marked by trauma (see Behar 1995; Bertharion 1998; Burgelin 1990; and van Montfrans 1999).

8. Here we are grateful to one of the readers to whom University Press of New En-gland/Dartmouth College Press assigned our manuscript for review. That reader sug-gested we clarify that, by privileging the formal virtue *of La disparition* and of film noir, we need not exclude the possibility that formal elision can give proof of trauma. By way of example, that reader notes that some of the most renown films noir utilize narrative tech-niques that neatly excise World War II: *The Killers* does so by establishing its two tempo-ral moments to either side of America's involvement in the war (the present moment in 1946 and the flashbacks in 1941); *Double Indemnity* manages to avoid any references to the war whatsoever, though it is planted firmly in the war years. To that list, we could add the scar on "The Swede's" (Burt Lancaster) hand in *The Killers* (see chapter 5); the implica-tion in *He Walked by Night* that Roy Morgan's (Richard Basehart) criminality might be born in part from what he suffered during the war; a similar suggestion in *Gun Crazy* that Bart Tare's (John Dall) time in the army might have aggravated his violent obsession with guns—all of these being narrative devices that allow these films to explore how characters who have been through traumatic situations behave later in life while sidestepping any focus on the traumatic event itself. In other words, we agree with this reader and do not want to suggest that the formal aspects of these narratives should be seen as *only* auto-exegetical mechanisms without any historical referent: this would be a doubly damning absence—the elision of these narratives' elisions. Rather, we would suggest the inverse. To claim that these formal constraints are only, or even primarily, about traumatic elision misses the various ways in which these narratives frame much more than an absence: they use formal devices, elision among them, to reflect upon their methods for telling a story.

9. Chandler's hard-boiled novels were among the works most often adapted by films noir, and it seems likely that Perec, in his admiration for American writers from Poe to midcentury mystery pulps, would have encountered Chandler as he crafted his own mysteries, *A Void* and *53 Days*.

10. The branch of literary studies known as narratology has developed precise terminology to discuss the "levels" of narration. The diegesis (adj. diegetic) is the level of the primary action within the narrative. If the narrator interrupts her story to comment upon it (e.g., "That was the day I learned a thing or two about telling a story, I can assure you"), that comment is considered as "extradiegetic." An imbedded story within a story occurs at the "hypodiegetic" level.

11. In literary studies, "exegesis" means a critical reading and explanation of a text (pl. exegeses). The term originally referred to a practice of interpreting religious scriptures (most commonly by decoding allegories) but has come to refer to any critical interpretation of a text. To say a text is "auto-exegetical" is to claim that it critically reads itself by commenting upon its own diegesis through hypo- or (more commonly) *extra*diegetic asides.

12. Thus, most readers understand *A Void* as a Holocaust narrative, and most viewers see noir as "dark" film in its style and themes. But as Johan Huizinga has demonstrated, humor need not be pigeonholed as either facetious or serious. It can be both at once and, indeed, much more. A better understanding of humor in this context would be the one foregrounded by Huizinga on the first page of the first chapter of his great study *Homo Ludens*: "[Play] is a *significant* function—that is to say, there is some sense to it. In play there is something 'at play' which transcends the immediate needs of life and imparts meaning to the action" (1955, 1).

13. In Georges Perec's *A Void*, some of the intertextual references include *Tristram Shandy*, *Moby Dick*, Edgar Allan Poe's "Purloined Letter," and Henry James's "The Figure in the Carpet."

14. For the purpose of this book, we selected films from our first thirty-two podcast episodes of *Out of the Past: Investigating Film Noir*, two of which were "double features" that investigated two films in relation to one another. Episode 11 compared *The Big Sleep* and *The Big Lebowski*, and Episode 30 involved *The Postman Always Rings Twice* and *The Man Who Wasn't There*. Thus, there were thirty-four films from which we could choose, but we decided not to use three of these: the resulting sample set consists of thirty-one films. The three episodes that didn't make the cut investigated *The Third Man*, *Reservoir Dogs*, and *The Black Dahlia*. *The Black Dahlia*, Brian De Palma's 2006 adaptation of James Ellroy's novel, didn't make the grade because ultimately it was not a particularly good neo-noir. *Reservoir Dogs* continues to intrigue us as a neo-noir, but we got caught up in a discussion of Tarantino and lost track of the noir qualities of the film. The exclusion of *The Third Man* is more revealing. It was the fourth episode of the podcast series, and it took time for us to understand how the various oulipian resonances (creative and critical) of our podcasts should play out in our conversations. We had a tendency early on to fall back on our disciplinary training. Clute examined *The Third Man* in terms of hard-boiled literature, and Edwards approached it via film studies. The result was a debate

over whether *The Third Man* was or was not film noir, and whether noir was a style or a genre, which produced very little new information of relevance to our current study. For a complete podcastography, see appendix 2.

15. As part of our podcast series, we started a list of "most requested films," and at some point in 2006 we began to consider films at the top of the fan-generated list. To this date, we still get requests from listeners for films to cover in the *Out of the Past* podcast.

16. See postliminary 2 for more information on the potential of user-generated databases in the study of film noir.

17. Regarding the idea of a homogenized iconography in critical studies of film noir, we would note that a limited pool of "standard-bearer" images recur in books on noir. To cite one common example, film stills highlighting the work of cinematographer John Alton predominate: frame enlargements (showcasing Alton's work from *The Big Combo,* for example) repeat in almost identical fashion throughout multiple books. This creates a familiarizing and homogenizing effect where a handful of widely reprinted images operate as synecdochic evidence for the noir style in general.

Chapter 2: One Hundred Thousand Billion Films Noir

1. Many of this new generation of filmmakers were Americans, such as Orson Welles and John Huston, but there were also a large number of émigré directors such as Billy Wilder, Jacques Tourneur, and Otto Preminger. This is discussed in detail in Hirsch 1981.

2. Another French critic who identified "noir" films in 1946 was Jean-Pierre Chartier. He is frequently cited in tandem with Nino Frank. (See Chartier 2003, 21–24.)

3. See Borde and Chaumeton [1955] 2002. In fairness, Borde and Chaumeton discuss and index a greater number of films in their study of film noir but include such notable noirs as *The Killers* and *Double Indemnity* under the categories of "Gangsters" and "Criminal psychology" respectively.

4. As James Naremore says in his introduction to a new edition of *Panorama,* in a delightful parenthetical, "(Film theorist Peter Wollen once remarked to me in conversation, not altogether facetiously, that the best way to describe film noir is to say that it is any movie described as noir by Borde and Chaumeton.)" (Naremore 2002, xiv).

5. One of the most extensive analyses of Borde and Chaumeton's *Panorama* can be found in James Naremore's chapter "History of an Idea" in *More than Night: Film Noir in Its Contexts* (2008, 9–39).

6. This point echoes claims made by James Naremore and Tom Conley. As Conley states, "The authors [Borde and Chaumeton] make an impressive inventory of film noir according to a model of evolution, roughly following Focillon's *Vie des Formes*" (1991, 237). For more on the academic roots and cosmogonic implications of Rabelais's lists, see Conley 1996.

7. In other words, Neale is placing the twenty-two films noir cited by Borde and Chaumeton into a numerical perspective—relative to the number of Hollywood film releases in the 1940s and 1950s—as a way of determining the dimensions of the noir canon. As Neale tabulates, "According to Joel Finler, 5,325 American films were released in the United States between 1940 and 1952, the period covered by Borde and Chaumeton. The

seven films mentioned by Frank, Rey and Chartier represent 0.13 per cent of this total, the 22 films in Borde and Chaumeton's core canon 0.41 per cent, and the 84 films they list overall 1.6 per cent" (2000, 146).

8. Paul Duncan's pocket-sized book is one of the more inclusive indices of film noir titles. His lists contain several categories that extend beyond American cinema, including "noir" films made in France, the United Kingdom, Italy, Mexico, and Japan. Duncan's list also contains films noir made after 1960 in two sections labeled "Post-Noir (1961–1975)" and "Neo-Noir (1976–1992)." (See Duncan 2003.)

9. Keaney's filmography also brings up the issue that the dates can differ from project to project, and that has profound effects. For example, Keaney's chronology of 1940–1959 completely subsumes Borde and Chaumeton's era. Keaney's comment about film viewing could be read as a rejoinder to Vernet's parenthetical comment about the plentitude of noir films (see chapter 1 of this book; Keaney 2003).

10. The unusual .5 source refers to eliminating duplicate references in two guides by Keaney, since Keaney is the only author repeated in the list of sources (see Keaney 2003, 2008).

11. Sidney further constrained his IMDb.com film noir search by date range (1950–1965), by language (English), and by type (no TV movies) to yield his result of 437 titles as of March 16, 2008. The Internet Movie Database (IMDb.com) makes an intriguing case around noir folksonomies/filmographies. Its list of films noir is constructed through fan votes and user-generated inputs. IMDb has indices of noir themes that have been collaboratively developed through the obsessive efforts of die-hard film noir fans.

12. Sidney, "Sidney's Film Noir Page," www.gaskcadd.com/ssk_pix/FilmNoir.htm (accessed February 12, 2010).

13. Issues of spectatorship and film viewing have encountered (and been impacted by) mathematics. One famous example is the role of mathematicians in the commercial sector of movie rentals. For several years, Netflix has had a contest that will award a million-dollar prize to anyone who can create "a movie-recommending algorithm 10 percent better" than the one Netflix currently uses (which is called "Cinematch"). The competition has attracted teams of mathematicians who have worked to improve the Netflix algorithm through the use of ever more complex mathematic formulas that "data mine" the Netflix database for bits of information that can more reliably predict what films a typical renter is likely to want to rent next based on their previous rental patterns. As *Wired Magazine* states, "The Netflix challenge is just one example of a kind of problem called *data mining*—trying to make useful sense out of a gigantic dataset, typically rather noisy, completely unintelligible to the naked eye, and, despite its size, often painfully incomplete." Digital humanities projects around "data mining" should consider how some of these corporate-driven algorithms influence questions of reception and spectatorship of film texts and, by extension, how algorithms might help researchers analyze these very same texts (Ellenberg 2008).

14. This book does not take up the noir vs. neo-noir debate. Some noir scholars believe that noir is a historical category, and the last films noir were made in the 1950s. For our purposes, we will consider films noir produced after 1958 as legitimate objects of noir study.

15. "Les mathématiques—plus particulièrement les structures abstraites des mathématiques contemporaines—nous proposent mille directions d'explorations, tant à partir de l'Algèbre (recours à de nouvelles lois de composition) que de la Topologie (considerations de voisinage, d'ouverture ou de fermature de texts)." Our translation is intended to call attention to the cartographic vocabulary in Le Lionnais's statement, for reasons that will become evident in chapter 4.

16. The use of computers as writing machines is a very oulipian idea, and for anyone who cares to read Queneau's sonnets, several websites are dedicated to electronic versions of *Cent mille milliards de poèmes*. One website, found at www.growndodo.com/wordplay /oulipo/10%5E14sonnets.html, allows users to generate a new sonnet with a simple "mouse-over." Over six hundred thousand versions of the sonnets have been electronically generated at this one site through January 2011.

17. We have decided to use the term "recombinatorial" in place of the more common "recombinant," because to our mind it places more emphasis on the importance of the act of writing. And as the Oulipo has stated, "C'est en écrivant sous contrainte que l'on devient écriveron sous contrainte." ("It is in writing under constraint that one becomes a writer under constraint.") It is interesting to note that the word *écriveron* is a neologism coined by Queneau, one that recalls conjugations of the verb *écrire* ("to write") and thus in its very morphology places the emphasis on process (within this statement, which likewise places the emphasis on process). (Oulipo, "L'introduction à l'usage des néophytes et des grands debutants," in Oulipo 2002, 7).

18. "Il faut encore remarquer qu'il était injuste de considérer les poèmes de Queneau comme 'la première oeuvre de littérature potentielle,' car la littérature potentielle existait avant la fondation de l'OuLiPo (c'est même ce que nous proposons de montrer ici). En revanche, ce que l'on peut affirmer sans grand risque d'erreur, c'est qu'elle constitue la première oeuvre de littérature potentielle *consciente*. Ou plutôt: *concertée*.

Concertée, oui, je préfère, car Raymond Queneau n'a pas la reputation de laisser 'l'inconscience' s'emparer de son écriture."

19. In the *Yale French Studies* article from which this quote is drawn, Roubaud further emphasizes the word "potentiality." The word itself appears in bold typeface and in a significantly larger font than the surrounding words, leaving no doubt as to the author's take on the potential of oulipian constraint.

20. The "exquisite corpse" (*cadavre exquis*) is a surrealist method where words or pictures are collectively assembled by chance. Participants of the game add a word or an image but do not know the other contributions until the end of the game, when a new aleatory assemblage is revealed to all participants.

21. Not for nothing does Queneau make a brief appearance in Naremore's story of surrealist Boris Vian, in the chapter "History of an Idea" in *More than Night*.

Chapter 3: Workshop of Potential Criticism

1. Le Lionnais, a founding member of the Oulipo, always anticipated that the group's workshops, procedures, and investigations would have resonances in other artistic domains. He invented the acronym, Ou-x-po, to signal a *potential* number of other groups,

where "x" signifies other types of creative fields and domains. Among the numerous Ou-x-pos in existence, there is an Oulipopo (Ouvroir de Littérature Policière Potentielle or Workshop of Potential Mystery Fiction), Oumupo (Ouvroir de Musique Potentielle, or Workshop of Potential Music), and even an Oucuipo (Ouvroir de Cuisine Potentielle, or Workshop of Potential Cooking). In this book, we are proposing an Oufinopo (Workshop of Potential Film Noir) and providing what we believe is the first sustained and substantial demonstration of the previously imagined Outcritpo (Workshop of Potential Criticism).

2. In this passage, Ray specifically states in a footnote, "In speaking of 'potential criticism,' I am thinking of the famous French avant-garde group OULIPO . . . whose members included Raymond Queneau, Italo Calvino, and Georges Perec." We will part company with Ray over this framing of the Oulipo as "avant-garde."

3. It is interesting to consider what Ray's approach would have looked like if he had actually developed a "potential criticism" based solely on oulipian procedures instead of surrealism. There is abundant evidence throughout his study to suggest that an oulipian approach would potentially have much to offer the discipline of film studies—a proposition we hope to consciously and conscientiously demonstrate in this book.

4. For more on this distinction, see the final pages of the preceding chapter.

5. This is a theme we explored in chapter 2 and that the founders of the Oulipo highlighted repeatedly: "Une autre idée bien fausse qui a également cours actuellement, c'est l'équivalence que l'on établit entre inspiration, exploration du subconscient et libération, entre hazard, automatisme et liberté. Or, *cette* inspiration qui consiste à obéir aveuglement à toute impulsion est en réalité un esclavage." ("Another very false idea is also making the rounds at the moment, and that is the equivalency between inspiration, exploration of the unconscious and liberation, between chance, automatism and freedom. But *this* sort of inspiration, which consists of blindly obeying every impulse, is in reality slavery.") (Calvino 1988, 123; translation ours).

6. Sheri Chinen Biesen makes an argument in ways compatible with Ray's reading of Andy Hardy: "Prototypes for film noir began appearing before America's entry into the war in December 1941. Influenced by earlier traditions, *noir* style was emerging by 1940 and 1941" (2005, 12).

7. "Art citationnel" is a term we will address in greater detail at the end of this chapter.

8. As a way to understand the power of the analytic tendency, one might consider the Oulipopo. The analytic Oulipopo "studied the situations and mechanisms that have been used in detective fiction, as well as the possible ways of combining them" (Oulipo 2005, 266). The analytic Oulipopo was anticipated by the publication of Le Lionnais's "Qui est le coupable?" ("Who Is Guilty?"), a study using algorithms to determine if there was a possible "guilty party" in detective fiction that had never been used before. After running through the various permutations, Le Lionnais believed he had found a new and unused potential: that the reader was the guilty party. While the exercise began with an analytic impulse, it quickly joined with the more "essential" Oulipian drive toward synthesis, aiming to "discover, distinguish, or invent procedures or constraints that could serve as 'aids to the imagination' of writers of detective stories" (Oulipo 2005, 255). Thus, once Le Lion-

nais's analytic combinatorics suggested a new possibility, that option was offered up as a constraint for writers to consciously utilize.

9. This is based on Mathew's own example of using four-letter words in his algorithm. For his sets of examples, see Mathews and Brotchie 2005, 184.

10. While the more common spelling of this word is nil, the *Oxford English Dictionary* defines nill (with two *l*'s) as "an instance of unwillingness; a disinclination for or aversion to something. Chiefly in collocation with *will*."

11. "[L'algorithme] serait capable de traiter les fragments des lettres—soit graphiques, soit phonétiques—et les composants de ceux-ci, pour ne pas parler d'amibes, d'atomes, et de quarks. Il pourrait s'adresser, au-delà des épisodes des fictions, aux livres entiers, aux literatures entières, aux civilizations, aux systèmes planétaires et solaires, aux galaxies—à tout ce qui en somme peut être maipulé sous sa forme materiélle ou symbolique."

12. This is by and large the tendency we saw in Robert Ray's gloss of the Oulipo.

13. It should come as no surprise that oulipian texts are auto-exegetical. In the very brief essay "Deux principes parfois respectés par les travaux oulipiens" ("Two principles sometimes respected by oulipian works"), the two principles are these: "Un texte écrit suivant une contrainte parle de cette contrainte; un texte écrit suivant une contrainte mathématisable contient les consequences de la théorie mathématique qu'elle illustre." ("A text written under constraint speaks of that constraint; a text written under a 'mathematicalizable' constraint contains the consequences of the mathematical theory that the constraint illustrates.") That more attention has not been given to these statements of the auto-exegetical qualities of oulipian texts is surprising, but it seems that perhaps critics have once again missed the tongue-in-cheek humor of oulipian writing and have taken it too literally at its word: these are not rules that are "sometimes respected" but rather rules that are always respected. It is just a question of whether they are respected to a greater or lesser degree. Thus, it is a question of how overtly a given oulipian text scripts auto-exegesis, not a question of *whether* it does so. (See Roubaud 1988, 90.)

14. "Il me semble . . . qu'on s'achemine vers un art qu'on pourrait dire 'citationnel,' et qui permet un certain progrès puisqu'on prend comme point de départ ce qui était un aboutissement chez les prédécesseurs. C'est un procédé qui me séduit beaucoup, avec lequel j'ai envie de jouer."

("It seems to me . . . that we are heading toward an art form that we could call 'citational,' and that permits a certain progress because we start from what was the end point for our predecessors. It is a process that really entices me, with which I want to play") (Perec 1998, 190–91). The full text of this interview was published in translation (Bénabou and Marcenac 1993).

15. For more on this argument, see Clute 2003. Motte is attuned to the ways that oulipian humor exceeds that of most texts and how it is one aspect of oulipian self-consciousness that should be carefully studied. He concludes the "Introduction" of *Oulipo: A Primer of Potential Literature* with a section entitled "Scriptor Ludens, Lector Ludens": "Even at its most polemical, even at its most ferociously doctrinaire, the Oulipo's work over the past twenty-five years has consistently been animated by a most refreshing spirit

of playfulness. The Oulipian text is quite explicitly offered as a game, as a system of ludic exchange between author and reader" (1986, 20). While we agree wholeheartedly with the first part of this statement, we would suggest that sometimes the oulipian text is offered as a ludic exchange between the author and his or her own writing (process and product). The reader is not always part of the equation.

16. These concepts were inspired in large part by the work of Tom Conley, whose course Cartographical Writing Clute had the pleasure of taking at Cornell, while Conley was in residence at the Cornell University Society for the Humanities/Andrew Dickson White House. In numerous publications, Conley demonstrates how representations of space in print or film texts enter into critical dialogue with the text in which they occur, creating both visible/narrative and ephemeral/self-reflexive topologies. (See Conley 1991, 1996, 2006).

Chapter 4: Build My Scaffolding High

The title of this chapter is a bilingual pun on the word "scaffolding." In French the word for scaffolding is "échafaudage." As Raymond Queneau has noted, to shape their language art, Oulipian authors construct a mathematically engineered "scaffolding" before spinning a tale, which is what we will do in the next chapter. But *échafaudage* also contains within it the word "échafaud," meaning "gallows." Thus the title of this chapter plays on "Build My Gallows High," the novel that served as the source for the 1947 Jacques Tourneur film, *Out of the Past*. There is also another layer of intertextual allusion, since this title recalls our podcast series on film noir, likewise called *Out of the Past*. And lastly, the pun is meant to elicit a playful bit of "gallows" humor, for in true oulipian fashion, one never knows what fate the scaffolding holds since it is built before it is put to its potential uses.

1. These tropes were particularly common in films noir, as we have discussed in our *Out of the Past* podcasts and will demonstrate in chapter 5 of this text.

2. Here we would credit Thompson with an exemplary act of plagiarism by anticipation of our Oufinopo, for he seems to possess extensive anticipatory knowledge of our argument. Or, to put it another way, by rediscovering his work through the anoulipistic activity of looking for precursors to our Oufinopo, we discover potentials already buried in his original work.

3. We do hope that our readers understand we are being tongue in cheek here, in particularly oulipian fashion.

4. Sheri Chinen Biesen's *Blackout: World War II and the Origins of Film Noir* is the most comprehensive archival examination of how wartime economic constraints and material restrictions affected the noir style. As Biesen explains, "Responding to extensive wartime cost-cutting measures, creative economizing affect[s] Hollywood *noir* film style. Hard-boiled icon Robert Mitchum once jested, 'Hell, we didn't know what film noir was in those days. We were just making movies. Cary Grant and all the big stars got all the lights. We lit our sets with cigarette butts.' Director Mark Robson recalled that in

shooting *The Seventh Victim* (1943) on a studio sound stage with recycled sets and back-lot streets 'the less light we put on them the better they looked'" (2005, 71).

5. Chapter 5 of this text demonstrates this tendency toward self-conscious borrowing with abundant visual evidence.

6. Vincent Camby, in his 1984 commentary on this film, refers to *Rope* as "a stunt to behold." Camby is extremely laudatory in his remarks on this particular Hitchcock film and sees the constraint as ultimately being very successful: "[Hitchcock's] obsession with telling a story without resorting to the usual methods of montage, and without cutting from one shot to another, results in a film of unusual, fascinating technical facility, whose chilliness almost perfectly suits the subject." However, as we have shown is so often the case with criticism surrounding formally constrained works, there is still an element of critical dismissiveness in Camby's depiction of this as a "stunt." Such critical framings of artificial constraints in fact "stunt" our appreciation of how constraint works to generate new potentials and how such constraints structure their own critical readings. Moreover, the critic's need to consider these constraints as "stunts" also underestimates the generative potential of constrained experiments and their subsequent impact on the development of art forms. One can't help but wonder if Hitchcock's "stunt" gave him new ideas for his later cinematic stories, and it could be a very useful exercise to watch Hitchcock's use of long takes in their post-*Rope* realization in such acknowledged masterworks as *Vertigo* and *Psycho* to see if these too bear the traces of constrained filmmaking.

7. In our podcast series, we have paid particular attention to the Coen brothers and their adaptation of classic films noir, authoring three double-length episodes that investigate the hard-boiled filmic and literary sources they have embraced. For more on these topics, please reference the original podcasts: episodes 11 (*The Big Sleep* and *The Big Lebowski*), 30 (*The Postman Always Rings Twice* and *The Man Who Wasn't There*), and 41 (*The Glass Key* and *Miller's Crossing*) are available at http://www.noircast.net/.

8. bst's approach to creating an "unbiased sample set" deserves further consideration in a book on oulipian approaches to film study. As they describe in their appendix A to *Classical Hollywood Cinema,* it would be impossible for them to watch all 29,998 feature titles made during the classic Hollywood era. Therefore, they decide they need a mathematical way to find, in their terms, an "unbiased sample" that doesn't rely on "personal preferences or conceptions of influential or masterful films" (1985, 388). bst use a method that would make Oulipians proud: they utilize the constraint of a random-number table to select 841 titles, and then attempt to find archival prints based on that new constrained set of films. As they relate, they are able to locate one hundred prints of these films in film archives and private collections. The goal is to get as close as possible to a mathematical "randomness" so their study can look at these one hundred texts as representative of the 29,998 feature films. It could be an interesting exercise to employ a similar constraint to achieve such a sample set of noir films from the extensive noir filmographies discussed in chapter 2, and could also (at least, potentially) be interesting to compare such an "unbiased" sample set with the thirty-one films we used in our study and then compare the noiremes inspired by each set. Such procedures are in keeping with oulipian "scaffolding,"

and clearly there are many potential ways to revitalize film noir criticism, and film studies in general, through the use of mathematics and constraint. Such experiments can always be run again with different sets of films—that is, different sets of constrained (and therefore representative) heterogeneous elements.

9. As examples of critics who see patterns of nonconformity in film noir, BST cite the film noir scholarship of E. Ann Kaplan, Raymond Borde and Etienne Chaumeton, Christine Gledhill, Paul Shrader, and Janey Place and Lowell S. Peterson.

10. To their credit, BST engage in the former maneuver, which most often seems devoid of any intent to disavow or appropriate the original auteur's genius.

11. No wonder then that the self-consciousness of *Touch of Evil* has been widely acknowledged.

12. "Les mathématiques—plus particulièrement les structures abstraites des mathématiques contemporaines—nous proposent mille directions d'explorations, tant à partir de l'Algèbre (recours à de nouvelles lois de composition) que de la Topologie (considerations de voisinage, d'ouverture ou de fermature de textes)" ("Mathematics—particularly the abstract structures of contemporary mathematics—propose a thousand directions for exploration, taking as a point of departure Algebra (recourse to new laws of composition) as much as Topology (considerations of proximity, opening or closure of texts)" (Le Lionnais 1973, 21; translation ours).

13. For more a more sustained reflection on how oulipian texts structure a critical commentary that is maplike, see chapter 4 of Clute's dissertation (2003), on Perec's use of François Rabelais's *Quart Livre.*

14. As J. P. Telotte puts it in his study *Voices in the Dark: The Narrative Patterns of Film Noir,* "Not since the days of film pioneers like Griffith, Thomas Ince, and William DeMille had the American cinema experienced such a fascination with the mechanics and the *possibilities* of storytelling (as in films noir)" (1989, 3; italics in original).

15. A good example of this point is raised by James Naremore in relation to a contemporary noir film by filmmaker David Lynch: *"Mulholland Dr.* is an impressive . . . proof, if any were needed, that a movie saturated with references to other movies can transcend or reanimate its basic material, turning it into a powerful form of art." *Mulholland Dr.,* as Naremore sees it, is based on a "complex system of rhymes, reversals, and mirror-image relations" (2008, 307). Given our analysis above, perhaps Naremore's conclusion should come as no surprise: "It is perhaps unimportant whether we give *Mulholland Dr.* a generic or stylistic label; but if we call it noir, and if film noir in its self-conscious, postmodern manifestations is occasionally capable of this kind of wrenching dramatic effect, then it remains capable of almost anything" (310).

16. The same might be said of neo-noir films, as is evident in the Coen brothers discussion of their first noir film, *Blood Simple:* "When people call *Blood Simple* a film noir, they're correct to the extent that we like the same kind of stories that people who made those movies liked. We tried to emulate the source that those movies came from rather than the movies themselves. *Blood Simple* utilizes movie conventions to tell the story. In that sense it's about other movies—but no more so than any other film that uses the medium

in a way that's aware that there's a history of movies behind it" (quoted in Erickson [1995] 1996, 321).

17. For an analogous argument, see chapter 3 of Clute's dissertation (2003), on critical reception of "The Purloined Letter" versus Perec's clever appropriation of the tale, and how that appropriation helps *A Void* structure auto-exegesis.

18. We might note that our podcasts somehow managed to convey our understanding of the ways these films explore and map their own topology, long before we had articulated our understanding in these terms. One listener, calling himself KM55, left the following review of our podcast series at iTunes: "These two guys do a great job reviewing noir and neo-noir films. They consistently provide unique, creative insights into the great movies in this dark corner of filmdom. Clute and Edwards are drawing a road map into the twisted world of film noir, film-by-film, and it's great fun taking the trip with them." We believe he gives us too much credit; we are in fact calling attention to the ways these films draw their own road map—thereby guiding our critical journey from the get-go.

19. J. P. Telotte has voiced a similar caution to critics but in even more oulipian terms: "*Noir,* after all, not only confronts us with the images and events that possess us as cultural beings, that weave us into their narrative; in the process, it also casts in relief the discursive practices that lead us to see ourselves as the creators, possessors, and narrators of these things. One result is that it reveals us as figures within the very fabric—of self and society—that we commonly weave. Another, more important one is that it warns us to take better care in that weaving, giving thought to the limitations of our loom" (1989, 35).

Chapter 5: Oufinopo

1. The story of the challenges we faced during this process occasions here an unavoidable tense shift, for which we beg our reader's pardon.

2. We feel that what we are doing in identifying noiremes is really an act of "describing never-before-noticed" aspects of familiar images—the very aspects that we become alert to if we train ourselves as "potential critics" whose job it is to try to be attuned to the textual moments that self-consciously call attention to themselves. A similar impulse guides critic Samuel Delany in his famous essay on "The Politics of the Paraliterary," where he argues for a new kind of criticism: "If, realizing the way in which the two meanings of definition (like the two meanings of art) create an unwinnable game of round-robin-chasing-after-one's-tail, critics of the paraliterary could retire the notion of definition once and for all, if they could restrict themselves to the far more modest-seeming task of describing our objects of concern (like comics, [science fiction], pornography . . .), describing never-before-noticed aspects, pointing out the most interesting examples, describing the myriad and fascinating ways in which those aspects react with one another and how they interact with readers and the world, we would produce a far less arrogant, far more interesting, far less self-crippling, and finally far more powerful criticism . . . than we usually do, a criticism that would go far further toward effecting the revolution in esthetic values that . . . I would like to see" (1999, 238).

3. Many film scholars view *The Maltese Falcon* as the first film noir, the film that created the stylistic template other films of the classic period would follow quite closely. It is

interesting to note that the running time of *The Maltese Falcon* is 100 minutes, 29 seconds. That our sample set averages such a similar running time seems to suggest not only that scholars have math on their side when they consider *The Maltese Falcon* as the template but also that the noir template had a "scientific" rigor based in part on the "formal logic of mathematics." Rather than thinking of noir in the surrealist vein as some filmic "écriture automatique" that reveals the unconscious of its author, it seems more fitting to see noir as constrained text that reveals a great deal about the interplay between constraint and narrative form. In other words, we believe noir was such a rich and productive movement precisely because it was, like oulipian texts, *so* constrained (constrained in ways that, the math would suggest, were *consciously* adopted). As Oulipians have argued, the more a constraint constrains, the more it liberates. That brings us back to our current study—this piece of constrained, *potential criticism*. We believe the fact that the average running time of our sample set came so close to that of *The Maltese Falcon* might also suggest that our unusual method for investigating these films is befitting.

4. For the purposes of this project, we did not go back to the celluloid reels of the films, which might have enabled us to do a similar procedure based on a precise number of film frames. Instead, all images used in this project were taken from DVD versions of the film using the software program VLC (http://www.videolan.org/vlc). The numbers we use for this project rely on the hours, minutes, and seconds from each of the DVDs as given by VLC. There might be some minor discrepancies between VLC's running times and the counters on some DVD players.

5. For the purposes of this project, we use the running time as designated by each of the DVDs. In a few instances, this number is slightly different from the running time of the film as listed in other film resources. It is beyond the scope of this project to get into debates about definitive running lengths and versions, such as with the ending of *Kiss Me Deadly* or *Touch of Evil*. In all cases, we relied on running time from the DVD copies we used for this project and the VLC software program.

Postscript

1. This quote, from *Alice in Wonderland,* is perfectly apropos an oulipian study. Lewis Carroll was both mathematician and novelist, and remains a favorite of many Oulipians. *Alice in Wonderland* is alluded to many times in *A Void.*

2. See postliminary 1 for more information on the podcast project.

3. "*Mutatis mutandis* is a Latin phrase meaning 'by changing those things which need to be changed' or more simply 'the necessary changes having been made.' The term is used when comparing two situations with a multiplicity of common variables set at the same value, in which the value of only one variable is allowed to differ—'all other things being equal'—thereby making comparison easier." Mutatis mutandis, Wikipedia, http://en.wikipedia.org/wiki/Mutatis_mutandis (accessed April 1, 2010).

4. Perec defended such moments of creative freedom (i.e., transgression), which Oulipians called the "clinamen" (taking the concept from Epicurean physics, via the pataphysicians), by quoting Paul Klee: "La génie, c'est l'erreur dans le système" ("Genius is the error in the system"). Of course, such a statement is tongue in cheek in a particularly

oulipian way, for clinamens (Perec's in particular) were anything but errors. See *Entretiens et conferences vol. II,* conference at the University of Copenhagen, October 29, 1981 (Paris: Joseph K.), 316. For the sake of posterity, the Oulipo also tried to give a (slightly) less tongue-in-check definition: "For Oulipians, the clinamen is a deviation from the strict consequences of a restriction. It is often justified on aesthetic grounds: resorting to it improves the results. But there is a binding condition for its use: the exceptional freedom afforded by the clinamen can only be taken on the condition that following the initial rule is still possible. In other words, the clinamen can only be used if it isn't needed. (A number of Oulipians, notably Italo Calvino, have felt that the clinamen plays a crucial role in Oulipian theory and practice)" (Oulipo 2005, 126).

Postliminary 1

1. RSS syndication, according to Dave Winer, who wrote the earliest versions of the software, stands for "real simple syndication." The authors concur with Winer's assessment that podcasting is a simple way to distribute audio content to audiences.

2. We are arguing that popular reach should not be discounted in academic work. The distinction between popular work and critical work needs to be reconsidered in the digital age, as work is increasingly being produced by scholars in new ways. The practice of blogging, for example, would fall into a category by which scholars can be quite popular and speak intelligently beyond the disciplinary boundaries established in higher education.

3. This is so despite the fact we have not promoted the shows or published new episodes regularly or frequently for nearly two years.

4. Bryan Alexander is doing this as part of his NITLE workshops on podcasting. These workshops are conducted on various campuses throughout the United States. See NITLE's website (www.nitle.org/) for more information on the workshops.

5. See "Film Noir," Wikipedia, http://en.wikipedia.org/wiki/Film_noir (accessed October 1, 2007). Perhaps the most prominent reference to our podcast is in the Wikipedia entry on *Murder, My Sweet,* which cites our debate on Dick Powell's performance as Marlowe.

6. Edwards was hired to teach new media in the Communication Department at Saint Mary's College of California. Clute was hired to teach French and Italian language and French literature in the Department of Modern Languages.

7. Shannon Clute and Richard Edwards, "Podcasting as Publication: Constructing a Serialized Academic Audiobook," paper presented at the NMC Online Conference on Personal Broadcasting, April 2006, http://archive.nmc.org/events/2006spring_online_conf (accessed April 1, 2010).

8. Their concerns were many, but two were principle. Should work that is peer warranted, postproduction, receive the same recognition and reward as work that is peer reviewed prepublication? Also, how would this work be archived and accessed by future scholars? We believe the answer to the first question is simply yes, for reasons Wikipedia has made clear. The second concern is valid, and we continue to work with librarians and new media scholars to find satisfactory answers and archiving solutions. Rank and Tenure's response made it clear that innovation comes at a price: it will likely be incumbent

upon innovators to justify new forms of scholarship within fairly static models for assessment, models designed by and for traditional print publication.

9. Yes, we are aware of the heavy-handedness of such rhetoric. And no, we are not growling as we write these lines. We agree with Mitchell's vision and imagine a fairly predictable fate probably awaits podcasting projects in the academy. Like most work that seems revolutionary at the time, podcasting will be respectable much sooner than we probably imagined and routinized as one more check box in a promotion and tenure file in the near future.

Postliminary 2

1. In this quote, Fournel uses the word "agm." Agms are defined as a "minimal unities of action or description." Noiremes would be analogous to the Paul Braffort and Georges Kermidjian term "agm" used by Fournel in describing the A.R.T.A. Project. It is worth noting that "unique" is our rendering of the word *particulière* in the original French, which might also be translated as particular, peculiar, private, special, singular, or personal (see Fournel 1998, 320; translation ours).

2. This terminology consciously echoes ideas prevalent in discussions of new media, forwarded by such thinkers as Lev Manovich and Janet Murray. In this instance, we are consciously recalling Murray's taxonomy of properties of the computer medium: participatory, procedural, encyclopedic, and spatial (see Murray 1997).

3. Of course, as Paul Fournel so aptly notes about the A.R.T.A. Project, these kinds of projects take "patience, work, and time (=money)." And the money part is no small element. Databases, such as the ones we suggest here, are still prohibitively expensive in the early part of the twenty-first century. While grants are available, they are still in limited supply, and most new work in the digital humanities is underfunded. But as digital trends have shown, those costs should come down over time.

4. However, the use of copyrighted material is still very problematic in online databases and continues to delimit media studies work in the digital humanities. It is likely existing intellectual property and copyright laws would work against a full realization of an online film noir database. Even at this early stage in its development, it is unclear whether the MTOE Project would even attract funding if it uses copyrighted material.

5. A not dissimilar project exists in the numerous websites that have created digital versions of Raymond Queneau's *Cent mille milliards de poèmes*. Most of these keep a running count of how many new combinations of the poem have been created by users on the Web.

6. "Toutefois, c'est en écrivant sous contrainte que l'on devient écriveron sous contrainte." ("It is in writing under constraint that one becomes a writer under constraint.") (See Oulipo, "L'introduction à l'usage des néophytes et des grands debutants," in Oulipo 2002, 7).

Further Readings

Selected Oulipian Works

For more information on the Oulipo

Oulipo: Abrégé de littérature potentielle. Translation ours. Turin, Italy: Editions Mille et Une Nuit, 2002.

Oulipo: Atlas de littérature potentielle. Saint-Amand, France: Editions Gallimard, 1981.

Oulipo: La littérature potentielle. Saint-Amand, France: Editions Gallimard, 1973.

Oulipo: A Primer of Potential Literature. Edited and translated by Warren Motte Jr. Normal, Ill.: Dalkey Archive, 1998.

The Oulipo Compendium. Edited and translated by Harry Mathews and Alastair Brotchie. London: Atlas Press, 2005.

Oulipo Laboratory: Texts from the Bibliothèque Oulipienne. Translated by Harry Mathews, Iain White, and Warren Motte Jr. London: Atlas Press, 1995.

For more information on the oulipian works mentioned in this book

ITALO CALVINO

"Cybernetics and Ghosts." In *The Uses of Literature,* translated by Patrick Creagh. New York: Harcourt Brace Jovanovich, 1982.

"How I Wrote One of My Books." In *Oulipo Laboratory: Texts from the Bibliothèque Oulipienne,* translated by Harry Mathews, Iain White, and Warren Motte Jr. London: Atlas Press, 1995.

If on a Winter's Night a Traveler. Translated by William Weaver. New York: Harcourt Brace Jovanovich, 1979.

"Prose and Anti-combinatorics." In *Oulipo: A Primer of Potential Literature,* edited and translated by Warren Motte Jr. Normal, Ill.: Dalkey Archive, 1998.

PAUL FOURNEL

"Computer and Writer: The Centre Pompidou Experiment." In *Oulipo: A Primer of Potential Literature,* edited and translated by Warren Motte Jr. Normal, Ill.: Dalkey Archive, 1998.

FRANÇOIS LE LIONNAIS

"LA LIPO (Le premier Manifeste)." In *Oulipo: La littérature potentielle.* Saint-Amand, France: Editions Gallimard, 1973.

"Who Is Guilty? [The Guilty Party]." In *The Oulipo Compendium,* edited and translated by Harry Mathews and Alastair Brotchie. London: Atlas Press, 2005.

HARRY MATHEWS
"L'algorithme de Mathews." In *Oulipo: Atlas de littérature potentielle.* Saint-Amand, France: Editions Gallimard, 1988.

GEORGES PEREC
A Void. Translated by Gilbert Adair. Boston: Verba Mundi, 1994.
La disparition. Paris: Editions Denoël, 1969.

RAYMOND QUENEAU
"A Hundred Thousand Billion Poems." Translated by Stanley Chapman. In *The Oulipo Compendium,* edited and translated by Harry Mathews and Alastair Brotchie. London: Atlas Press, 2005.
Cent mille milliards de poèmes. Afterword by François Le Lionnais. Paris: Gallimard, 1961.

References

Barthes, Roland. 1989a. *Roland Barthes.* Translated by Richard Howard. Berkeley: University of California Press.

———.1989b. *The Rustle of Language.* Translated by Richard Howard. Berkeley: University of California Press.

Behar, Stella. 1995. *Georges Perec: Écrire pour ne pas dire.* New York: Peter Lang.

Bénabou, Marcel. 2001. "Quarante siècles d'Oulipo." *Magazine Littéraire* 398 (2001): 20–26.

Bénabou, Marcel, and Bruno Marcenac. 1993. "Georges Perec Owns Up: An Interview with Marcel Bénabou and Bruno Marcenac." Translated by David Bellos. *Review of Contemporary Fiction* 13 (1) (Spring): 17–20.

Bens, Jacques. 1981. "Queneau Oulipian." In *Oulipo: Atlas de littérature potentielle.* Paris: Editions Gallimard.

Bertharion, Jacques-Denis. 1998. *Poétique de Georges Perec: ". . . une trace, une marque ou quelques signes."* Paris: A.-G. Nizet.

Biesen, Sheri Chinen. 2005. *Blackout: World War II and the Origins of Film Noir.* Baltimore: Johns Hopkins Press.

Borde, Raymond, and Étienne Chaumeton. [1955] 2002. *A Panorama of American Film Noir 1941–1953.* Translated by Paul Hammond. San Francisco: City Light Books.

Bordwell, David, Janet Staiger, and Kristin Thompson. 1985. *The Classical Hollywood Cinema: Film Style and Mode of Production to 1960.* New York: Columbia University Press.

Bould, Marc. 2005. *Film Noir: From Berlin to Sin City.* New York: Wallflower.

Brook, Vincent, and Allen Campbell. 2003. "Pansies Don't Float: Gay Representability, Film Noir, and *The Man Who Wasn't There.*" *Jump Cut* 46.

Burgelin, Claude. 1990. *Georges Perec.* Paris: Edition du Seuil.

Calvino, Italo. 1979. *If on a Winter's Night a Traveler.* Translated by William Weaver. New York: Harcourt Brace Jovanovich.

———.1982. "Cybernetics and Ghosts." In *The Uses of Literature,* translated by Patrick Creagh. New York: Harcourt Brace Jovanovich.

———.1988. "Multiplicity." In *Six Memos for the Next Millennium,* translation ours. New York: Vintage International.

———.1995. "How I Wrote One of My Books." In *Oulipo Laboratory: Texts from the Bibliothèque Oulipienne,* translated by Harry Mathews, Iain White, and Warren Motte Jr. London: Atlas Press.

———.1998. "Prose and Anti-combinatorics." In *Oulipo: A Primer of Potential Literature,* edited and translated by Warren Motte Jr. Normal, Ill.: Dalkey Archive.

Camby, Vincent. 1984. "Hitchcock's 'Rope': A Stunt to Behold." *New York Times,* June 3.

Camus, Albert. 1991. *The Myth of Sisyphus and Other Essays.* Translated by Justin O'Brien. New York: Knopf.

Casper, Drew. 2007. *Postwar Hollywood, 1946–1962.* New York: Blackwell.

Chandler, Raymond. 1995. "*The Long Goodbye.*" In *Raymond Chandler: Later Novels and Other Writings.* New York: Library of America.

Chartier, Jean-Pierre. 2003. "Americans Are Also Making Noir Films." In *Film Noir Reader 2,* edited and translated by Alain Silver and James Ursini. New York: Limelight.

Clément, Catherine. 1979. "Auschwitz, ou la disparition." *L'Arc* 76:87–90.

Clute, Shannon. 2003. *The Last Laugh: Punning and Plagiary in Georges Perec's* La Disparition. PhD diss., Cornell University. Ann Arbor, Mich.: University Microfilms International (3104435).

Clute, Shannon, and Richard Edwards. 2006. "Podcasting as Publication: Constructing a Serialized Academic Audiobook." Paper presented at the NMC Online Conference on Personal Broadcasting, April. http://archive.nmc.org/events/2006spring_online_conf (accessed April 1, 2010).

Conley, Tom. 1991. *Film Hieroglyphs: Ruptures in Classical Cinema.* Minneapolis: University of Minnesota Press.

———.1996. *The Self-Made Map: Cartographic Writing in Early Modern France.* Minneapolis: University of Minnesota Press.

———.2006. *Cartographic Cinema.* Minneapolis: University of Minnesota Press.

Consenstein, Peter. 2002. *Literary Memory, Consciousness, and the Group Oulipo.* Netherlands: Faux Titre.

Delany, Samuel. 1999. "Politics of the Paraliterary." In *Shorter Views: Queer Thoughts and the Politics of the Paraliterary.* Middletown, Conn.: Wesleyan University Press.

Dimendberg, Edward. 2004. *Film Noir and the Spaces of Modernity.* Cambridge, Mass.: Harvard University Press.

Duncan, Paul. 2003. *Film Noir: Films of Trust and Betrayal.* North Pomfret, Vt.: Trafalgar Square Publishing.

Durgnat, Raymond. 1996. "Paint It Black: The Family Tree of the Film Noir." In *Film Noir Reader,* edited by Alain Silver and James Ursini. Pompton Plains, N.J.: Limelight Editions.

Eco, Umberto. 1984. "Postscript." In *The Name of the Rose.* New York: Harcourt.

Ellenberg, Jordan. 2008. "This Psychologist Might Outsmart the Math Brains Competing for the Netflix Prize." *Wired Magazine,* February 25. www.wired.com/techbiz/media/magazine/16-03/mf_netflix (accessed March 24, 2010).

Entretiens et conferences vol. II. 1981. Conference at the University of Copenhagen, October 29. Paris: Joseph K.

Erickson, Todd. [1995] 1996. "Kill Me Again: Movement Becomes Genre." In *Film Noir Reader,* edited by Alain Silver and James Ursini. Pompton Plains, N.J.: Limelight Editions.

Fournel, Paul. "Odinateur et Écrivain, L'Éxpérience du Centre Pompidou." In *Oulipo: Atlas de littérature potentielle.* Paris: Editions Gallimard, 1988.

Frank, Nino. [1946] 2003. "A New Kind of Police Drama: The Criminal Adventure." In *Film Noir Reader 2,* edited and translated by Alain Silver and James Ursini. New York: Limelight.

Gide, Andre. 1952. "The Evolution of the Theater." In *My Theater: Five Plays and an Essay.* New York: Knopf.

Grant, John. 2006. *Noir Movies: Facts, Figures and Fun.* London: AAPPL Artists and Photographers Press.

Hammett, Dashiell. [1929] 1992. *The Maltese Falcon.* New York: Vintage Crime/Black Lizard.

Hirsch, Foster. 1981. *The Dark Side of the Screen: Film Noir.* New York: Da Capo Press.

———. 1999. *Detours and Lost Highways: A Map of Neo-noir.* New York: Limelight Editions.

Huizinga, Johan. 1955. *Homo Ludens: A Study of the Play Element in Culture.* Boston: Beacon Press.

Huston, John. [1941] 2004. The Maltese Falcon: *The Shooting Script.* Alexandria, Va.: Alexander Street Press.

Jameson, Fredric. 1993. "Synoptic Chandler." In *Shades of Noir,* edited by Joan Copjec. New York: Verso.

Kaplan, E. Ann, ed. 1998. *Women in Film Noir.* London: BFI Publications.

Keaney, Michael F. 2003. *Film Noir Guide: 745 Films of the Classic Era, 1940–1959.* Jefferson, N.C.: McFarland.

———. 2008. *British Film Noir Guide.* London: McFarland and Company.

Kerr, Paul. [1979] 1996. "Out of What Past? Notes on B Film Noir." In *Film Noir Reader,* edited and translated by Alain Silver and James Ursini. Pompton Plains, N.J.: Limelight Editions.

———. 1983. "My Name Is Joseph H. Lewis." *Screen* 24 (4–5): 48–67.

Krutnik, Frank. 1991. *In a Lonely Place: Film Noir, Genre, Masculinity.* New York: Routledge.

LeJeune, Phillipe. 1991. *La mémoire et l'oblique: Georges Perec autobiographe.* Paris: P.O.L.

Le Lionnais, François. 1973. "LA LIPO (Le premier Manifeste)." In *Oulipo: La littérature potentielle,* translation ours. Saint-Amand, France: Editions Gallimard.

———. 1986. "Second Manifesto." In *Oulipo: A Primer of Potential Literature,* edited and translated by Warren Motte Jr. Normal, Ill.: Dalkey Archive.

———. 2005. "Who Is Guilty? [The Guilty Party]." In *The Oulipo Compendium,* edited and translated by Harry Mathews and Alastair Brotchie. London: Atlas Press.

Lescure, Jean. 1973. "Petite histoire de l'Oulipo." In *Oulipo: la littérature potentielle.* Saint-Amand, France: Editions Gallimard.

Lowenthal, Marc. 2000. *Raymond Queneau: Stories and Remarks.* Lincoln: University of Nebraska Press.

Magoudi, Ali. 1996. *La Lettre Fantôme.* Paris: Les Editions de Minuit.

Martin, Richard. 1997. *Mean Streets and Raging Bulls: The Legacy of Film Noir in Contemporary American Cinema*. Lanham, Md.: Scarecrow Press.

Mathews, Harry. 1988. "L'algorithme de Mathews." In *Oulipo: Atlas de littérature potentielle*. Saint-Amand, France: Editions Gallimard.

Mathews, Harry, and Alastair Brotchie, eds. 2005. *The Oulipo Compendium*. London: Atlas Press.

Mayer, Geoff, and Brian McDonnell. 2007. *Encyclopedia of Film Noir*. Westport, Conn.: Greenwood Press.

McBride, Joseph. 2006. *Whatever Happened to Orson Welles? A Portrait of an Independent Career*. Lexington: University Press of Kentucky.

Mitchell, W. J. T. 1995. "Interdisciplinarity and Visual Culture." *Art Bulletin* 77 (4): 540–44.

Monaco, James. 2004. *The New Wave: Truffault, Godard, Chabrol, Rohmer, Rivette*. New York: Oxford University Press.

Motte, Warren, Jr. 1986. "Introduction." In *Oulipo: A Primer of Potential Literature*, edited and translated by Warren Motte Jr. Lincoln: University of Nebraska Press.

———. 2006. "Raymond Queneau and the Early Oulipo," *French Film Forum* 31 (1): 41–54.

Muller, Eddie. 1998. *Dark City: The Lost World of Film Noir*. New York: St. Martin's Griffin.

Murray, Janet. 1997. *Hamlet on the Holodeck: The Future of Narrative in Cyberspace*. New York: Free Press.

Naremore, James. 2002. "A Season in Hell." In *A Panorama of American Film Noir 1941–1953*, edited by Raymond Borde and Étienne Chaumeton. Translated by Paul Hammond. San Francisco: City Light Books.

———. 2008. *More than Night: Film Noir in Its Contexts*. 2nd ed. Berkeley: University of California Press.

Neale, Stephen. 2000. *Genre and Hollywood*. London: Routledge.

Oulipo. 1973. *Oulipo: La littérature potentielle*. Saint-Amand, France: Editions Gallimard.

———. 1988. *Oulipo: Atlas de littérature potentielle*. Saint-Amand, France: Editions Gallimard.

———. 1995. *Oulipo Laboratory: Texts from the Bibliothèque Oulipienne*. Translated by Harry Mathews, Iain White, and Warren Motte Jr. London: Atlas Press.

———. 1998. *Oulipo: A Primer of Potential Literature*, edited and translated by Warren Motte Jr. Normal, Ill.: Dalkey Archive.

———. 2002. *Oulipo: Abrégé de littérature potentielle*. Translated ours. Turin, Italy: Editions Mille et Une Nuit.

———. 2005. *The Oulipo Compendium*, edited and translated by Harry Mathews and Alastair Brotchie. London: Atlas Press.

Perec, Georges. 1969. *La disparition*. Paris: Editions Denoël.

———. 1994. *A Void*. Translated by Gilbert Adair. Boston: Verba Mundi.

———. 1998. *Un homme qui dort*. Paris: Editions Gallimard.

Place, Janey, and Lowell Peterson. [1974] 1996. "Some Visual Motifs of Film Noir." In *Film Noir Reader,* edited and translated by Alain Silver and James Ursini. Pompton Plains, N.J.: Limelight Editions.

Polan, Dana. 1986. *Power and Paranoia: History, Narrative, and the American Cinema, 1940–1950.* New York: Columbia University Press.

———. 1993. *In a Lonely Place* (BFI Film Classics). London: BFI.

Queneau, Raymond. 1961. *Cent mille milliards de poèmes.* Afterword by François Le Lionnais. Paris: Gallimard.

———. 2005. "A Hundred Thousand Billion Poems." Translated by Stanley Chapman. In *The Oulipo Compendium,* edited and translated by Harry Mathews and Alastair Brotchie. London: Atlas Press.

Ray, Robert B. 1998. *The Avant-Garde Finds Andy Hardy.* Cambridge, Mass.: Harvard University Press.

———. 2001. *How a Film Theory Got Lost and Other Mysteries in Cultural Studies.* Bloomington: Indiana University Press.

Roubaud, Jacques. 1988. "Deux principes parfois respectés par les travaux oulipiens." In *Oulipo: Atlas de littérature potentielle.* Paris: Editions Gallimard.

———. [1991] 2005. "The Oulipo and Combinatorial Art." In *The Oulipo Compendium,* edited and translated by Harry Mathews and Alastair Brotchie. London: Atlas Press.

———. 2004. "Perecquian OULIPO." Translated by Jean-Jacques Poucel. Pereckonings: Reading Georges Perec. *Yale French Studies* 105:99–109.

Schatz, Thomas. 1981. *Hollywood Genres.* Boston: McGraw-Hill.

Schrader, Paul. [1972] 1996. "Notes on Film Noir." In *Film Noir Reader,* edited and translated by Alain Silver and James Ursini. Pompton Plains, N.J.: Limelight Editions.

Seaman, Bill. 2000. "Recombinant Poetics vs. Oulipo." Paper delivered at CaiiA Conference in Paris. http://projects.visualstudies.duke.edu/billseaman/textsOulipo.php (accessed April 1, 2010).

Silver, Alain. 1996. "Introduction." In *Film Noir Reader,* edited and translated by Alain Silver and James Ursini. Pompton Plains, N.J.: Limelight Editions.

Silver, Alain, and Elizabeth Ward, eds. 1992. *Film Noir: An Encyclopedic Reference to the American Style.* Woodstock, N.Y.: Overlook Press.

Telotte, J. P. 1989. *Voices in the Dark: The Narrative Patterns of Film Noir.* Chicago: University of Illinois Press.

Thompson, John O. 1992. "Dialogues of the Living Dead." In *Classical Hollywood Narrative: The Paradigm Wars,* edited by Jane M. Gaines. Durham, N.C.: Duke University Press.

Van Montfrans, Manet. 1999. *Georges Perec: La Contrainte du Réel.* Amsterdam: Rodopi.

Vernet, Marc. 1993. "Film Noir on the Edge of Doom." In *Shades of Noir: A Reader,* edited by Joan Copjec. New York: Verso.

Welles, Orson, and Peter Bogdanovich. 1992. *This Is Orson Welles.* Edited by Jonathan Rosenbaum. New York: Harper Collins.

Index

Johansson, Scarlett, 272
Johnson, Rian, xvii

Kahn, Janine, 19
Kantor, MacKinlay, 268
Kaplan, E. Ann, 8
Kaufman, Boris, 273
Kazan, Elia, 177, 191, 273
Keaney, Michael F., 14, 283n9
Kellaway, Cecil, 203, 274
Kermidjian, Georges, 293n1
Kerr, Paul, 33, 36
Killers, The (1946): in Borde and Chaumeton's *A Panorama of American Film Noir, 1941–1953*, 282n3; filmography, 270; "Frenchman's question and the Swede's answer" noireme in, 116–17; "golden harps" noireme in, 194–95; "mirror and the blind man" noireme in, 200–201; "money is no insurance" noireme in, 146–47; "moving too fast" noireme in, 54–55; podcastography, 278; staircase trope in, 245; World War II excised in, 280n8
Killing, The (1956): "academy of chumps and suckers" noireme in, 158–59; filmography, 270–71; "not fair" noireme in, 228–29; podcastography, 278; "probability of a poodle" noireme in, 240–41; "voice of God" noireme in, 100–101
King, Sherwood, 271
Kiss Kiss Bang Bang (2005), 38, 277
Kiss Me Deadly (1955): "erotic and neurotic" noireme in, 58–59; filmography, 271; guide books weighted toward films like, 15; "hammering hero" noireme in, 218–19; "irresistible danger" noireme, 242–43; "LA

absurd" noireme in, 192–93; "look deep" noireme in, 132–33; podcastography, 277
Klee, Paul, 291n4
Kline, Benjamin H., 266
Krasker, Robert, 77
Krasner, Milton R., 275
Kroeger, Berry, 268
Kruger, Otto, 273
Krutnik, Frank: on film noir criticism, 3, 13, 279n1; on generic unity of film noir, 11; *In a Lonely Place*, 7, 11; on scholarship versus pleasure in film noir, 3
Kubrick, Stanley, 101, 159, 241, 270

"LA absurd" noireme, 192–93
Lady from Shanghai, The (1947): "cut and dyed" noireme in, 72–73; filmography, 271; "on trial" noireme in, 216–17; podcastography, 278; "sharks in the water" noireme in, 196–97
Lady in the Lake, The (1947), 67, 99
Lamarr, Hedy, 10
Lancaster, Burt, 55, 117, 195, 201, 270, 280n8
Lang, Fritz, 107, 139
Langella, Frank, 143, 268
LaShelle, Joseph, 272
Laszlo, Ernest, 133, 193, 267, 271
Latis, 279n2
Laura (1944): filmography, 271–72; Frank includes in film noir, 12; inclusion in this study, 9; "noir atmosphere" noireme in, 124–25; "playing with the theme" noireme in, 198–99; podcastography, 278; "under a harsh glare" noireme in, 208–9; "undercover" noireme in, 204–5

noireme in, 140–41; in *Out of the Past* podcast, 281n14; podcastography, 278; self-conscious constraints in, 39

March, Joseph Moncure, 275

March of Times newsreels, 103

Marlowe, Philip (character): *The Big Sleep,* 95, 121, 137, 251, 265; *Murder, My Sweet,* 75, 83, 151, 153, 183

Marshman, D. M., Jr., 275

Martin, Richard, 13

Masterson, Whit, 276

Maté, Rudolph, 57, 175, 267

mathematics: formal mathematical logic in Perec's *A Void,* 32; movie-recommending algorithms, 283n13; Oulipo's interest in, 5, 17, 18, 26, 43; recombinatorial poetics, 18, 19, 284n17

Mathews, Harry: on constraint, 30; Mathews's Algorithm, 26–29, 42, 46–47; on potential in Oulipo, 17; on potential reading, 21, 29–30, 37, 47, 255

Mazurki, Mike, 83, 273

McDormand, Frances, 141, 272

Meeker, Ralph, 59, 219, 271

Melville, Herman, 32

Metro-Goldwyn-Mayer (MGM): *The Asphalt Jungle,* 264; *The Postman Always Rings Twice,* 9, 85, 274

Metropolis (1926), 107

Metty, Russell, 276

Millan, Victor, 179, 187

Miller's Crossing (1989), 38–39, 277

Miramax Films: *The Grifters,* 268

"mirror and the blind man" noireme, 200–201

mise en abyme, 189

Mitchell, Thomas, 270

Mitchell, W. J. T., 260–61

Mitchum, Robert, 65, 155, 181, 215, 274, 287n4

Möhner, Carl, 275

"money is no insurance" noireme, 146–47

Monroe, Marilyn, 135

Moore, Julianne, 265

Motte, Warren, 29, 30, 42, 279n1, 286n15

movie rentals, 15–16, 283n13

"moving too fast" noireme, 54–55

MTOE ("Maltese Touch of Evil") Project, 262–63

Mulholland Dr. (2001), 289n15

Muller, Eddie, xvii, 277

Mulvey, Laura, 8

Murch, Walter, 63, 276

Murder, My Sweet (1944): "blind man's view" noireme in, 74–75; "Chandler's Marlowe" noireme in, 150–51; filmography, 273; Frank includes in film noir, 12; "noir in the head" noireme in, 182–83; podcastography, 278; "Powell's Marlowe" noireme in, 152–53; "shots in the city" noireme in, 82–83

Murray, Janet, 293n2

Murrow, Edward R., 103, 143

Musuraca, Nicholas, 105, 269, 274

Myth of Sisyphus, The (Camus), 117, 195

Name of the Rose, The (Eco), 33, 255

Naremore, James, 7, 13, 16, 93, 282n4, 284n21, 289n15

Neal, Tom, 93, 267

Neale, Stephen, 13, 16, 282n7

"needing a gun" noireme, 70–71

Neeson, Liam, 265

neo-noir: *Blade Runner,* 81, 107; color palette in, 69; as emulating the sources, 289n16; inclusion in this study, 9, 283n14; in lists of film noir, 14, 16

Netflix, 15–16, 283n13

New Criticism, 260

New Media Consortium, 259

"news on noir" noireme, 102–3

newsreels, 103

Nicholson, Jack, 99, 165, 237, 266

Noël, Magali, 139

"noir atmosphere" noireme, 124–25

"noir camp" noireme, 166–67

"noir color" noireme, 68–69

noiremes, 46–48; database of, 263; how they were written, 255–56

"noir entendres" noireme, 120–21

"noir in the head" noireme, 182–83

"noir shoots stars" noireme, 78–79

Nolan, Christopher, 107, 221, 264

"nooses and nets" noireme, 148–49

nostalgia, 249

"not fair" noireme, 228–29

Notorious (1946): filmography, 273; "noir shoots stars" noireme in, 78–79; podcastography, 278; staircase trope in, 245

"Nouveau genre 'policier,' Un: L'aventure criminelle" (Frank), 12

O'Brien, Edmond: *D.O.A.,* 57, 175, 267; *The Hitch-Hiker,* 105, 269; *The Killers,* 147, 270

Oldman, Gary, 265

Olmos, Edward James, 266

Olson, Nancy, 275

O'Neil, Bob, 276

On the Waterfront (1954): "artful and artless" noireme in, 190–91; filmography, 273–74; "flipside of noir" noireme in, 176–77; podcastography, 278

"on trial" noireme, 216–17

"open is closed" noireme, 122–23

Oucritpo (Workshop of Potential Criticism), 22, 26

Oufinopo (Workshop of Potential Film Noir), xvii, 22, 35, 287n1

Oulipo (Ouvroir de Littérature Potentielle), xv–xvi; *anoulipism,* 5, 22, 26, 30, 263; auto-exegesis of texts of, 6, 43, 286n13; versus the avant-garde, 23, 25; Carroll as favorite of, 291n1; on clinamens, 291n4; computer-based operations in, 4, 280n4, 284n16; on constraint, 6, 8, 24, 46, 284n17, 291n3; film noir compared with, 34, 35, 39, 43; humor in, 6, 286n15; interest in mathematics, 5, 17, 18, 26, 43; intertextual borrowing in, 37; members of, 279n2; on plagiarism by anticipation, 6, 8, 21–32, 35; on potential, 6, 8, 17–18, 23, 26; Queneau's *Cent mille milliards de poèmes* in history of, 18; Ray on critical theory and, 24–25; scholarly approaches to, 6, 41; self-consciousness in, 10, 41, 43, 46; surrealism contrasted with, 19, 25, 285n5; *synoulipism,* 4–5, 22, 26, 30, 263; systematic and scientific approach of, 4

Oulipopo, 285n1, 285n8

Out of the Past (1947): "caught" noireme in, 154–55; filmography, 274; "flutter of curtains" noireme in, 181; *Gun Crazy* compared with, 215; "into the countryside" noireme in, 64–65; Mathews's Algorithm applied to, 28–29; in *Out of the Past* podcast, 257; podcastography, 278; as quintessential noir, 12

Out of the Past: Investigating Film Noir podcast, 257–61; on films drawing their own road maps, 290n18; films selected for, 8–9, 281n14; number of downloads, 258; podcastography, 277–78; as source of "investigative notes" of this study, 255–56; as unraveling the canvas of film noir, xvii

ouvroir: digitally accessible, 263; meanings of, xv; Oulipo, xv–xvi; as workshop, xvi

Ouvroir de Littérature Potentielle. *See* Oulipo (Ouvroir de Littérature Potentielle)

Panorama of American Film Noir, 1941–1953, A (Borde and Chaumeton), 12–14, 282n3

Paramount Pictures: *Chinatown,* 266; *Double Indemnity,* 267; *Sunset Blvd.,* 9, 161, 275

Pathé Consortium Cinéma: *Du rififi chez les hommes,* 274–75

Paxton, John, 273

peer review, 257, 259, 261

Peoples, David, 266

Perec, Georges: art citationnel of, 26, 30–31, 32, 37; and Chandler, 281n9; on clinamens, 291n4; Mathews as friend of, 27; in Oulipo, xvi, 279n2; parents of, 31; personal experience in works of, 280n7; Ray compared with, 26. See also *Void, A* (*La disparition*) (Perec)

Peters, Jeffrey, xvii, 277

Peterson, Lowell, 35, 245

Pfister, Wally, 264

Phillips, Scott, xvii

Pickup on South Street (1953), 277

Place, Janey, 35, 245

"players" noireme, 168–69

"playing with the theme" noireme, 198–99

podcasting, 257

"Podcasting as Publication: Constructing a Serialized Academic Audiobook," 259

podcastography, 277–78

Poe, Edgar Allan, 32, 44

"point of view" noireme, 98–99

Polanski, Roman, 69, 99, 165, 237, 266

police procedurals, 131, 133, 189

Polito, Jon, 272

Polygram Filmed Entertainment: *The Big Lebowski,* 265

Postman Always Rings Twice, The (1946): filmography, 274; "framed" noireme in, 202–3; "glamour noir" noireme in, 84–85; inclusion in this study, 9; "open is closed" noireme in, 122–23; in *Out of the Past* podcast, 281n14; podcastography, 278

post—September 11, 2001, culture, 221

potential: constraints' creative, 36–39, 47, 48; criticism, 22, 23, 25, 26, 262, 285n3, 291n3; Oucritpo (Workshop of Potential Criticism), 22, 26; Oulipo on, 6, 8, 17–18, 23, 26. *See also* potential reading

potential reading: Mathews on, 21, 29–30, 37, 47, 255; and Perec's *A Void,* 32

Powell, Dick, 75, 83, 151, 153, 183, 273

"Powell's Marlowe" noireme, 152–53

Preminger, Otto, 12, 125, 139, 199, 271, 282n1
Price, Vincent, 209, 272
"probability of a poodle" noireme, 240–41
Producers Releasing Corporation (PRC): *Detour,* 266–67; films included in this study, 9
production values, 35–36

Queneau, Raymond: *Cent mille milliards de poèmes,* 17–18, 19, 284n16, 293n15; on constraint, 24; early surrealism of, 19; *écriveron,* 284n17; on inspiration, 19, 26; on mathematics, 18; in Oulipo, xvi, 279n2
Queval, Jean, 279n2
"Qui est le coupable?" (Le Lionnais), 285n8

Rabelais, François, 13, 32
Raiders of the Lost Ark (1981), 243
Rains, Claude, 273
Raksin, David, 199
"random element" noireme, 104–5
Ray, Robert, 22–26; alphabetic studies of, 24; on Barthes on Proust, 24; on Oulipo and critical theory, 24–25; on potential criticism, 23, 285n2
recombinatorial poetics, 18, 19, 284n17
Red Scare, 163
Reed, Carol, 231
Reed, Donna, 213, 270
Reinhardt, Betty, 272
Reservoir Dogs (1992), 278, 281n14
Rififi (1955). See *Du rififi chez les hommes* (1955)
Riis, Jacob, 111
RKO Radio Pictures: *The Hitch-Hiker,*

61, 269; *It's a Wonderful Life,* 269–70; *Murder, My Sweet,* 273; *Notorious,* 273; *Out of the Past,* 274; *The Set-Up,* 275
Roache, Linus, 107
Roberts, Roy, 269
Robinson, Edward G., 91, 147, 267
Robson, Mark, 287n4
Rocky (1976), 235
Rodman, Howard, xvii, 277
"roller coaster" noireme, 214–15
Rope (1948), 38, 287n6
Rosson, Harold, 264
Roubaud, Jacques: in Oulipo, xvi, 279n2; "The Oulipo and Combinatorial Art," 18–19; on Queneau's *Cent mille milliards de poèmes,* 18, 284n19; on two principles respected in oulipian works, 286n13
Rouse, Russell, 267
"rub of the ear" noireme, 136–37
"running out of time" noireme, 66–67
running time percentage (RTP), 47–48, 49
Ruskin, Harry, 274
Ryan, Robert, 67, 235, 275

Saint, Eva Marie, 177, 191, 274
Savage, Ann, 267
Scavengers, The (1959), 16
Schatz, Thomas, 42
Schmidlin, Rick, 276
Schmidt, Albert-Marie, 279n2
Schulberg, Budd, 273
Scorsese, Martin, 145
Scott, Ridley, 81, 111, 266
Seitz, John F., 267, 275
Selby, Spencer, 14
self-consciousness: in *Chinatown,* 99; constraint and, 38–39; in *Detour,* 93;

Tetzlaff, Ted, 273
They Live by Night (1949), 277
Thieves' Highway (1949), 277
Thin Man, The (1934), 209
Third Man, The (1949): *The Asphalt Jungle* compared with, 77; *He Walked by Night* compared with, 231; *Hitch-Hiker* compared with, 105; in *Out of the Past* podcast, 278, 281n14
Thompson, Jim, 109, 268, 270
Thompson, John O., 34–35, 287n2
Thompson, Kristin, 39–41, 288n8
Thornton, Billy Bob, 141, 272
Tierney, Gene, 125, 199, 205, 209, 272
"time and crime" noireme, 184–85
time constraints, 47, 290n3
"time for a new protagonist" noireme, 96–97
Tirez sur la pianiste (1960), 37
Tobias, George, 275
"to the point" noireme, 60–61
Totter, Audrey, 275
Touch of Evil (1958): "blowing up noir" noireme in, 62–63; "bull outside the ring" noireme in, 222–23; constraint and, 38, 288n6; "double, crossed" noireme in, 178–79; filmography, 275–76; "if you are mean enough to steal from the blind, help yourself," 45, 173; as last classical film noir, 63; low-budget cinematography in, 35; as "noir's rococo tombstone," 43; podcastography, 278; restored version of, 63, 275–76; self-consciousness of, 63, 289n11; self-reflexive puns in, 63, 173, 179, 187; "slightest separation" noireme in, 232–33; "stealing from the blind" noireme in, 172–73; in title of this study, 10; "upon reflection"

noireme in, 186–87; "we're closed" noireme in, 126–27
Tourneur, Jacques, 12, 257, 274, 282n1
Towne, Robert, 237, 266
transcriptum, 256
Travers, Henry, 270
Trevor, Claire, 273
trial sequences, 217
tribute shots, 36, 103
Truffaut, François, 37
Trumbo, Dalton, 215, 268
Turner, Lana, 85, 123, 203, 274
Tuska, Jon, 14
Twentieth Century Fox: *Laura*, 9, 271–72

Ulmer, Edgar G., 36, 93, 266
"under a harsh glare" noireme, 208–9
"undercover" noireme, 204–5
underscore music, 235
United Artists: *D.O.A.*, 267; *Gun Crazy*, 268–69; *The Killing*, 270–71; *Kiss Me Deadly*, 271
Universal International Pictures: *Touch of Evil*, 275–76
Universal Pictures: *The Killers*, 270
"upon reflection" noireme, 186–87
"upper hand" noireme, 112–13
Ursini, James, 7

Valentine, Paul, 65
Varney, Bob, 276
Veiller, Anthony, 270
Vernet, Marc, 1, 2–3
"vertical bars" noireme, 86–87
Vickers, Martha, 95, 265
Vidor, Charles, 73
"voice of God" noireme, 100–101
voice-overs, 38, 46, 83, 91, 101, 153

Don't look back, baby. Don't *ever* look back.

—*The Strange Love of Martha Ivers* (1946)

Interfaces: Studies in Visual Culture

EDITORS MARK J. WILLIAMS AND ADRIAN W. B. RANDOLPH,
DARTMOUTH COLLEGE

This series, sponsored by Dartmouth College Press, develops and promotes the study of visual culture from a variety of critical and methodological perspectives. Its impetus derives from the increasing importance of visual signs in everyday life, and from the rapid expansion of what are termed "new media." The broad cultural and social dynamics attendant to these developments present new challenges and opportunities across and within the disciplines. These have resulted in a transdisciplinary fascination with all things visual, from "high" to "low," and from esoteric to popular. This series brings together approaches to visual culture—broadly conceived—that assess these dynamics critically and that break new ground in understanding their effects and implications.

For a complete list of books that are available in the series, visit www.upne.com.